D1624442

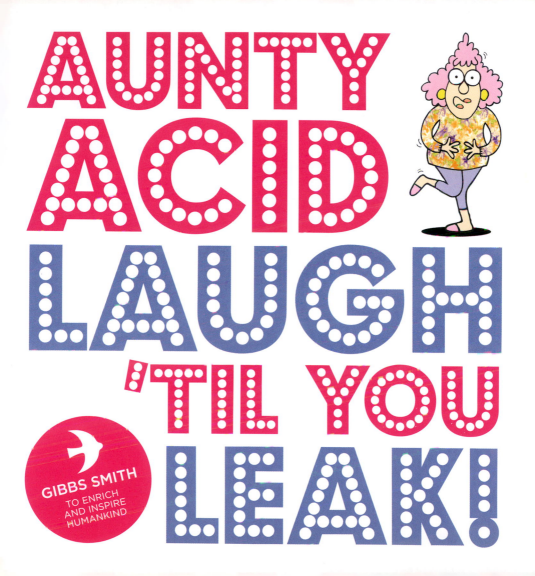

AUNTY ACID
LAUGH 'TIL YOU LEAK!

GIBBS SMITH
TO ENRICH
AND INSPIRE
HUMANKIND

Dear Beloved Reader,

Sorry to interrupt you. I'm sure you're positively thrilled to have your hands on my new book and can't wait to lock yourself in the little ladies' room, closet or wherever your favorite place to hide from your family is—and get stuck in!

I just need to warn you in advance that the following pages contain some of my all-time best gags, one-liners and side-splitting wisecracks, so watch out for the following side effects:
ROFL (rolling on the floor laughing)
LYAO (laughing your ass off)
or worst of all—LTYL (laughing 'til you leak).

Should you develop any of the symptoms above, put the book down immediately and go do something super boring and serious...the dusting, perhaps— or, in extreme cases, fold your laundry.

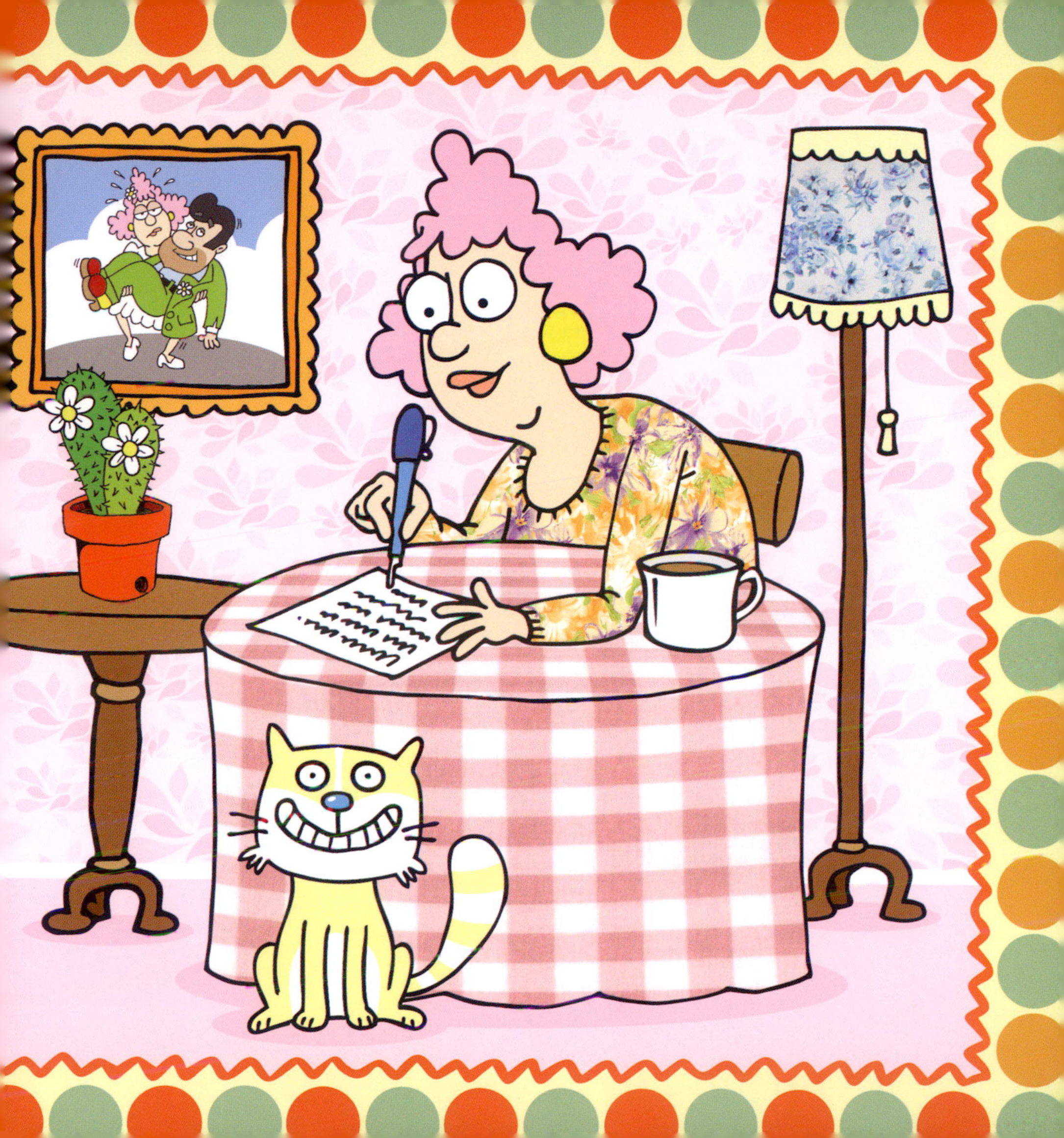

MODERN
L·I·F·E

Man has created the wheel....
Man has landed on the moon....
You can now video call someone
on the other side of the world!

It seems like
they've got an app
or a gadget for
everything these
days, so why am I
still waiting for a
freakin' mute
button for
humans? Huh?

I guess the person who called it a mobile phone didn't anticipate us lying on the sofa, covered in crumbs, scrolling through Facebook, did they?

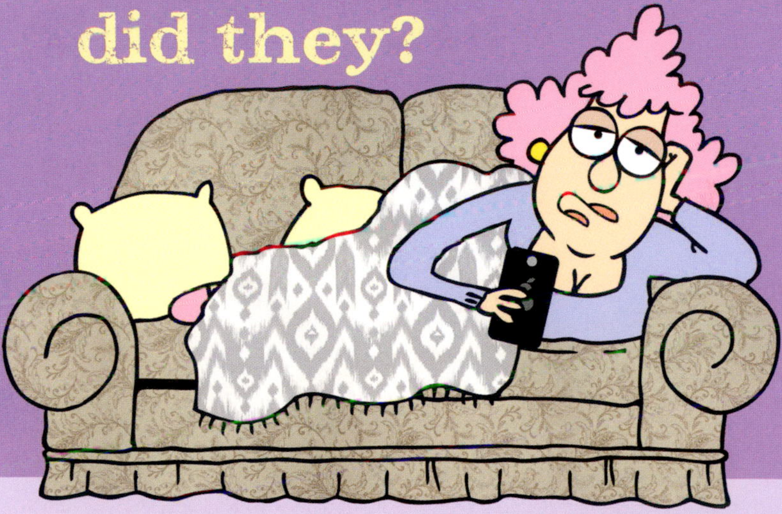

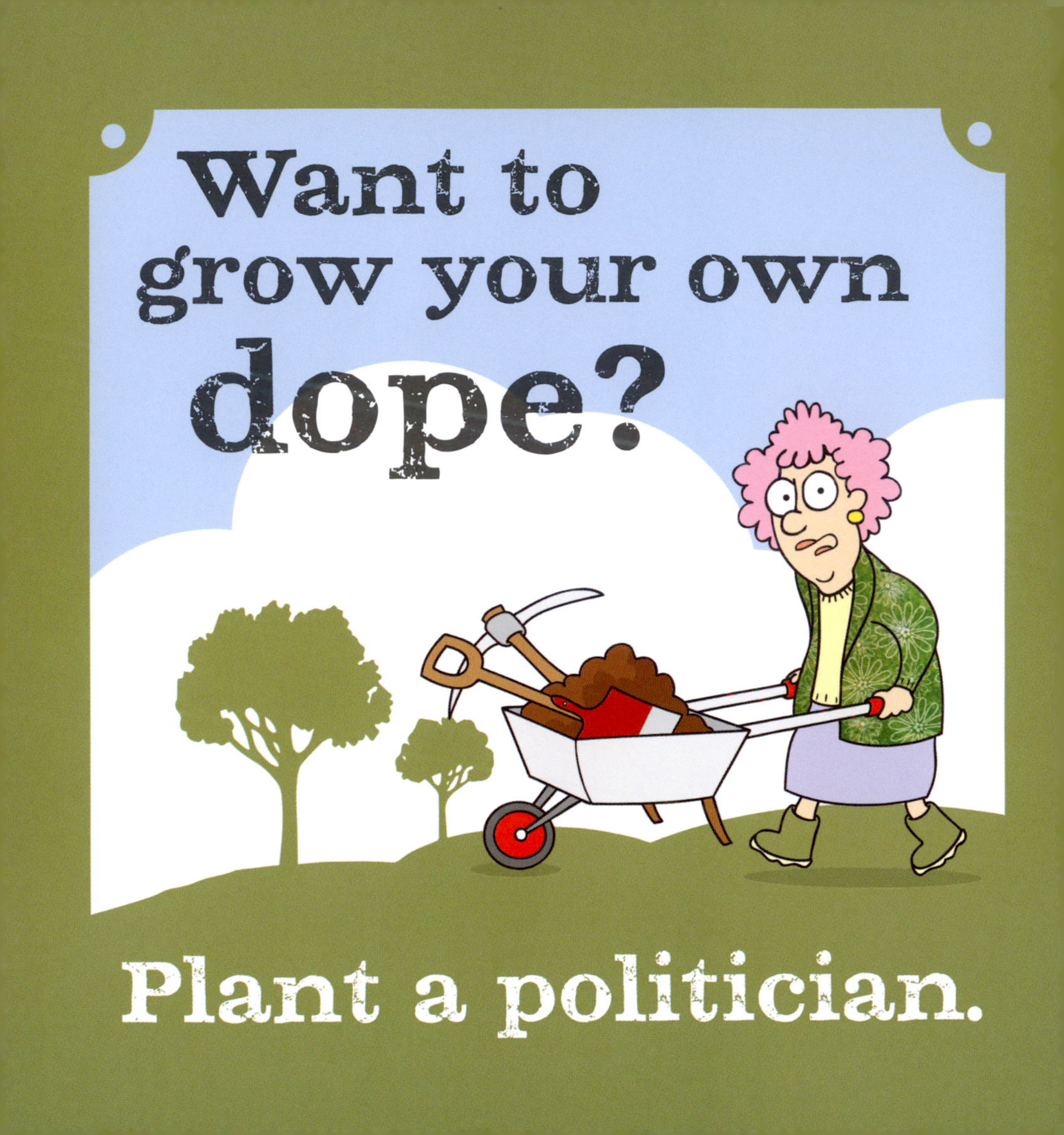
Want to grow your own dope?
Plant a politician.

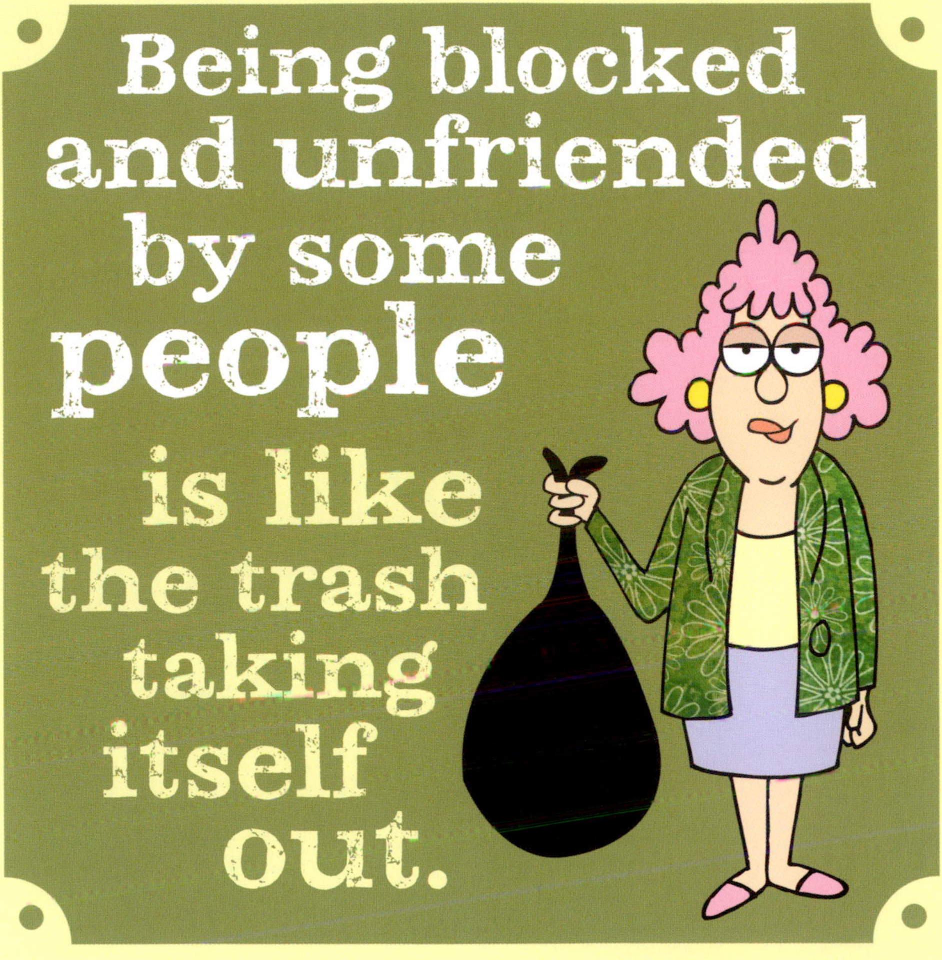
Being blocked and unfriended by some people is like the trash taking itself out.

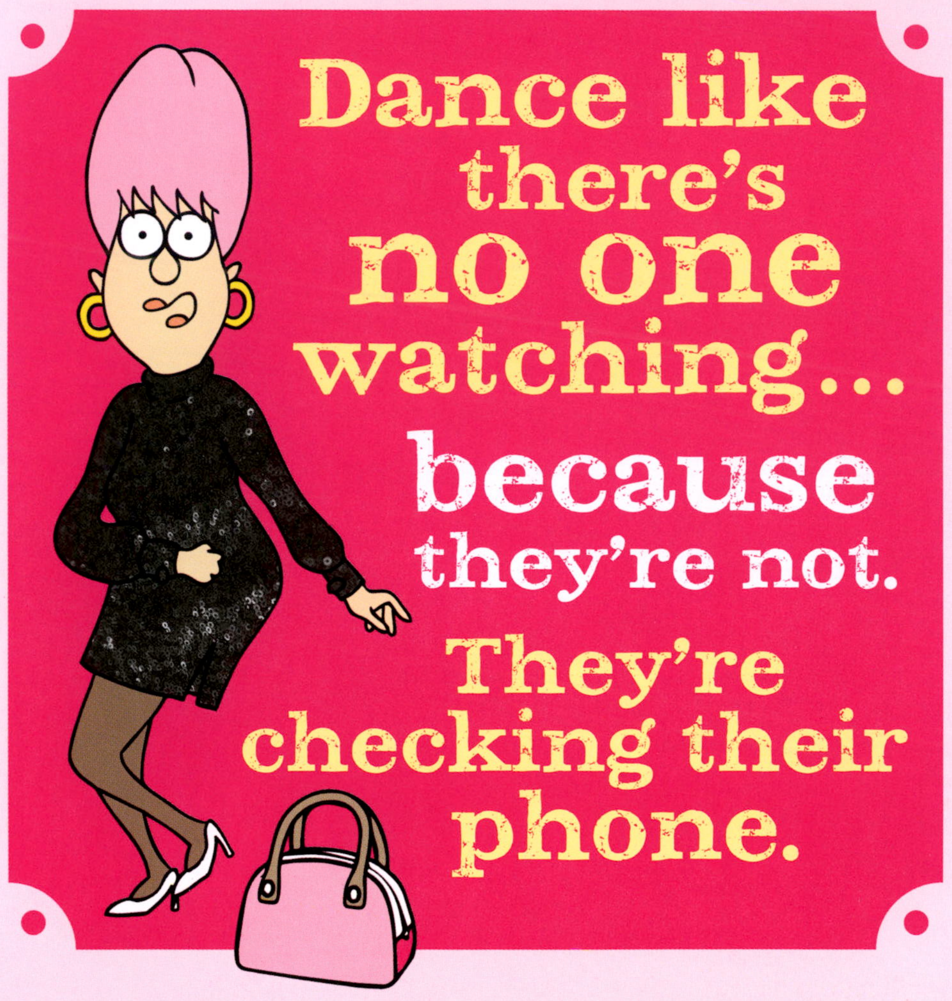

Dance like there's **no one** watching...

because they're not.

They're checking their phone.

Computer keys I'd like to be able to use in real life:

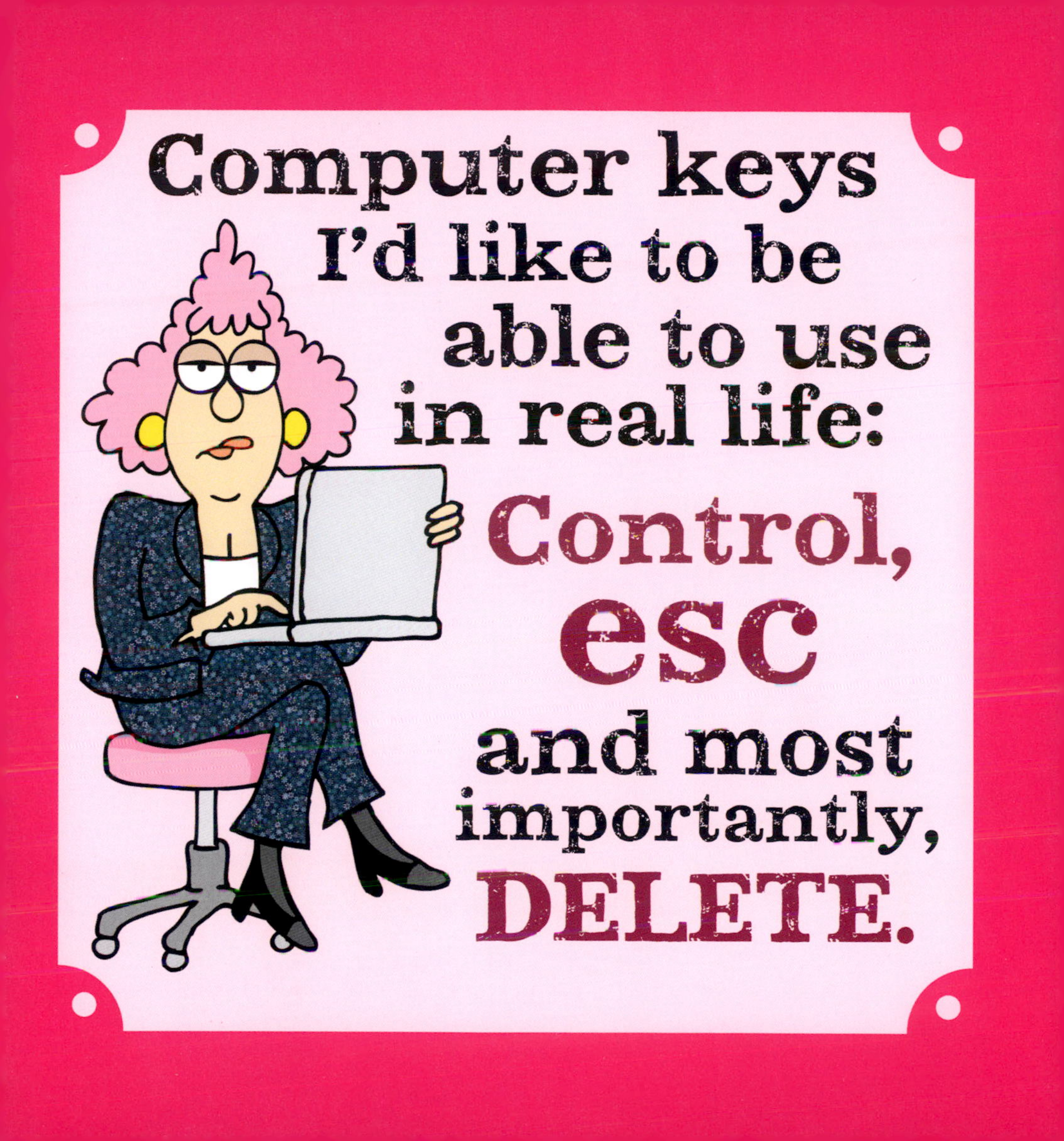

Control, esc and most importantly, DELETE.

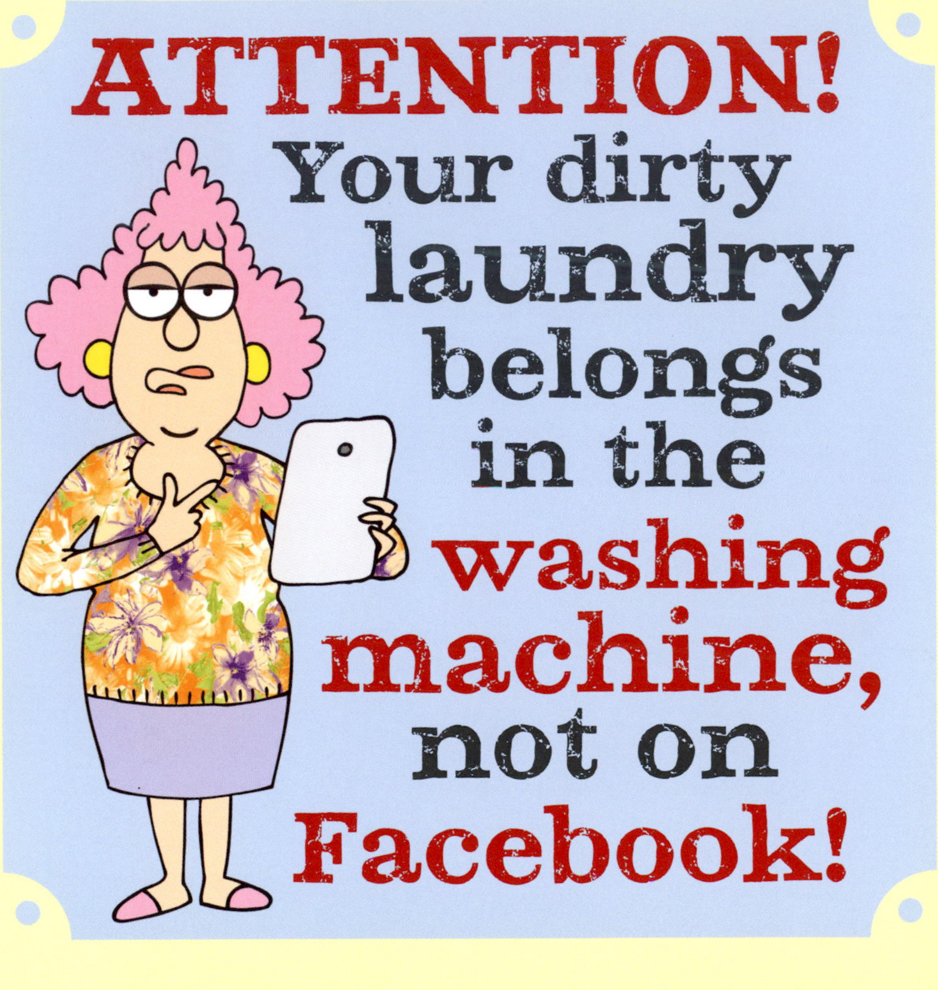
ATTENTION!
Your dirty laundry belongs in the washing machine, not on Facebook!

Never ask Google for medical advice!

I've gone from mild headache to clinically dead in 3 clicks.

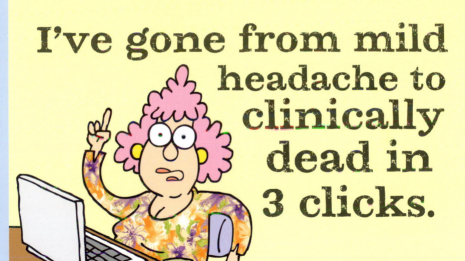

STUPID freakin’ PEOPLE

Brains are awesome…I wish everybody had one! I mean, they say ignorance is bliss, but for the rest of us, it’s a pain in the freakin’ ass! These days, common sense must be worth more than gold ’cause it’s definitely the rarest of all the natural resources. I can only assume that the stupid people were put here to test my anger management skills (and I’m failing). If you also find your inner monologue is mostly annoyed sighs, then you might need to sit down, take a few deep breaths, and read on for my favorite laughs on that all too familiar subject of **stupid freakin’ people.**

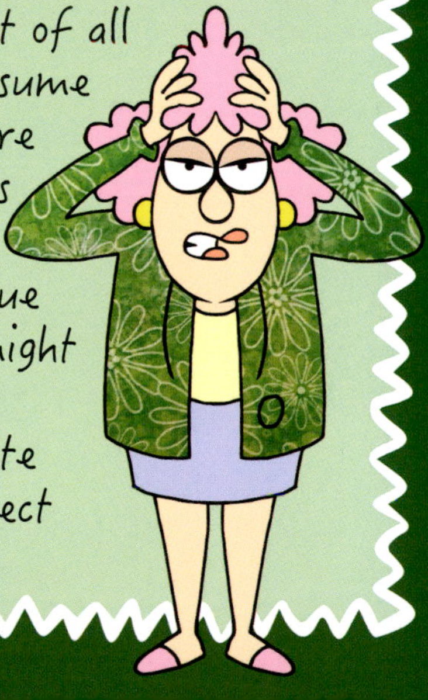

Hey, you'd better grab your **DUMBRELLA.** It's really stupid out there today.

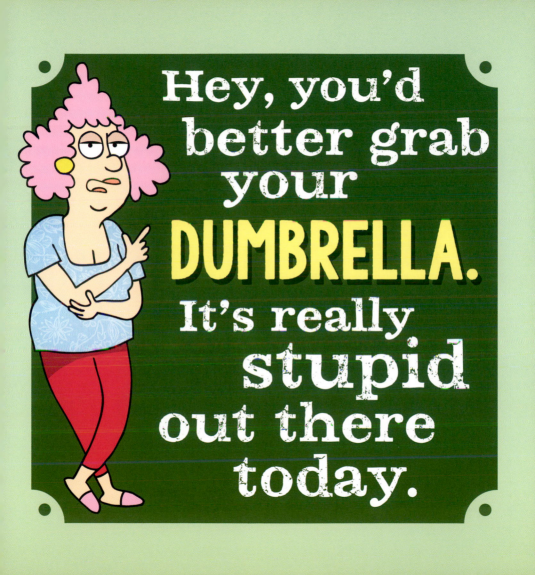

YES, I AM A MEMBER OF THE

CSI TEAM:

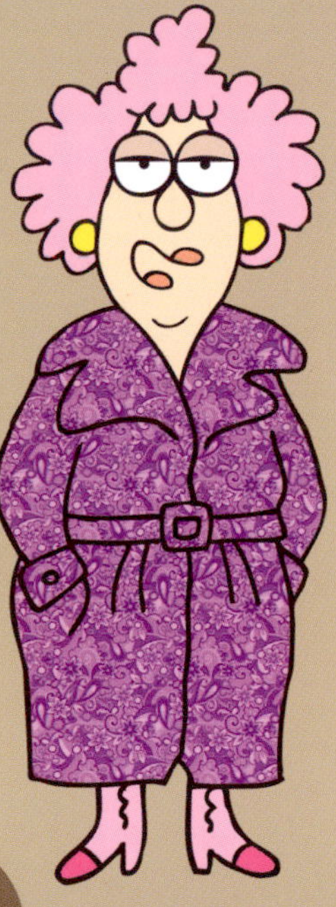

CAN'T STAND IDIOTS.

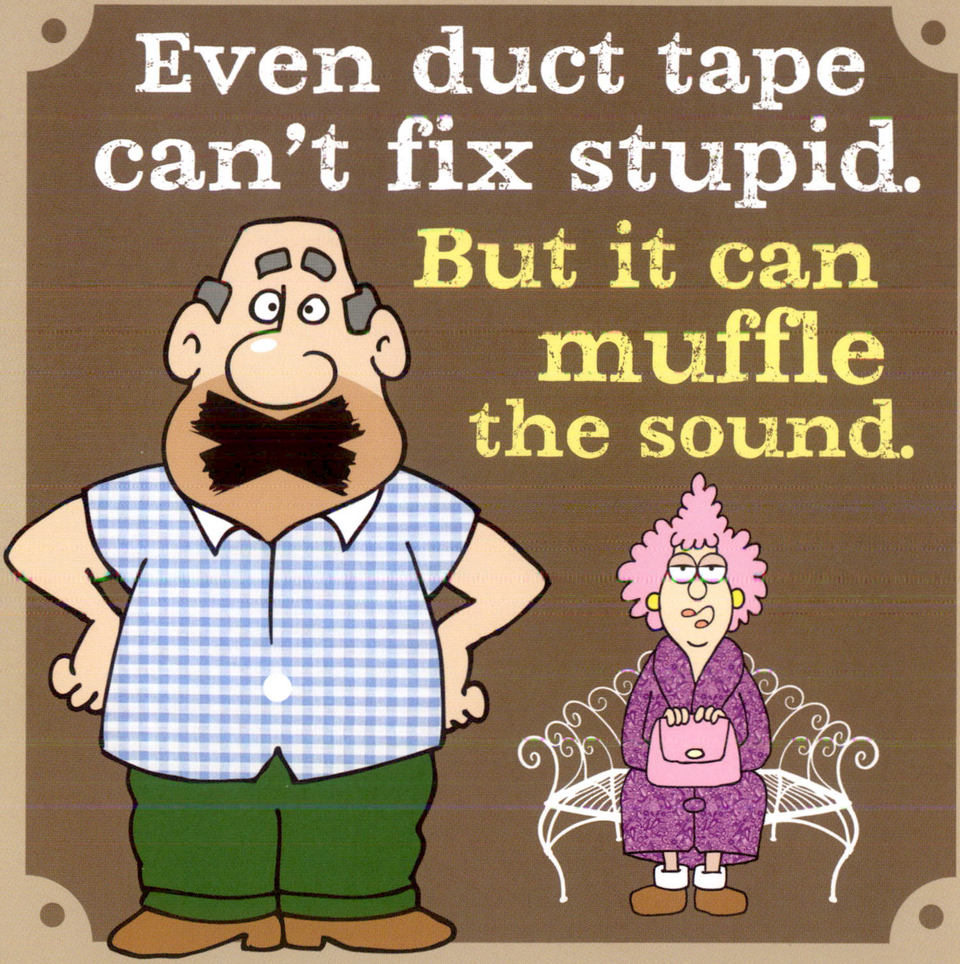
Even duct tape can't fix stupid.
But it can muffle the sound.

There are no
stupid
questions

...but there are
lots of
inquisitive
idiots!

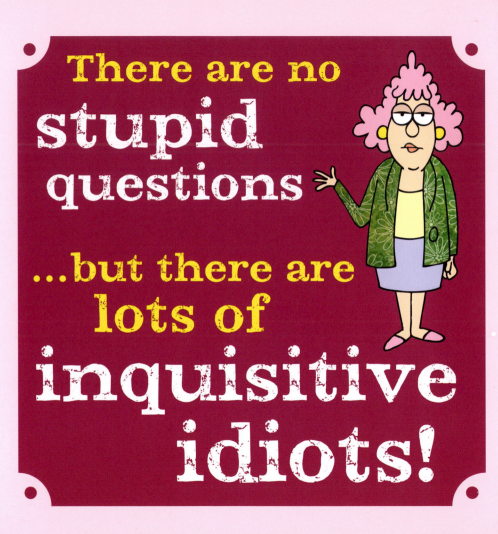

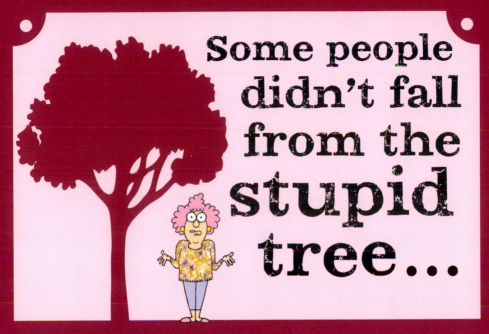

Some people didn't fall from the **stupid tree**...

They were dragged through the entire dumbass forest.

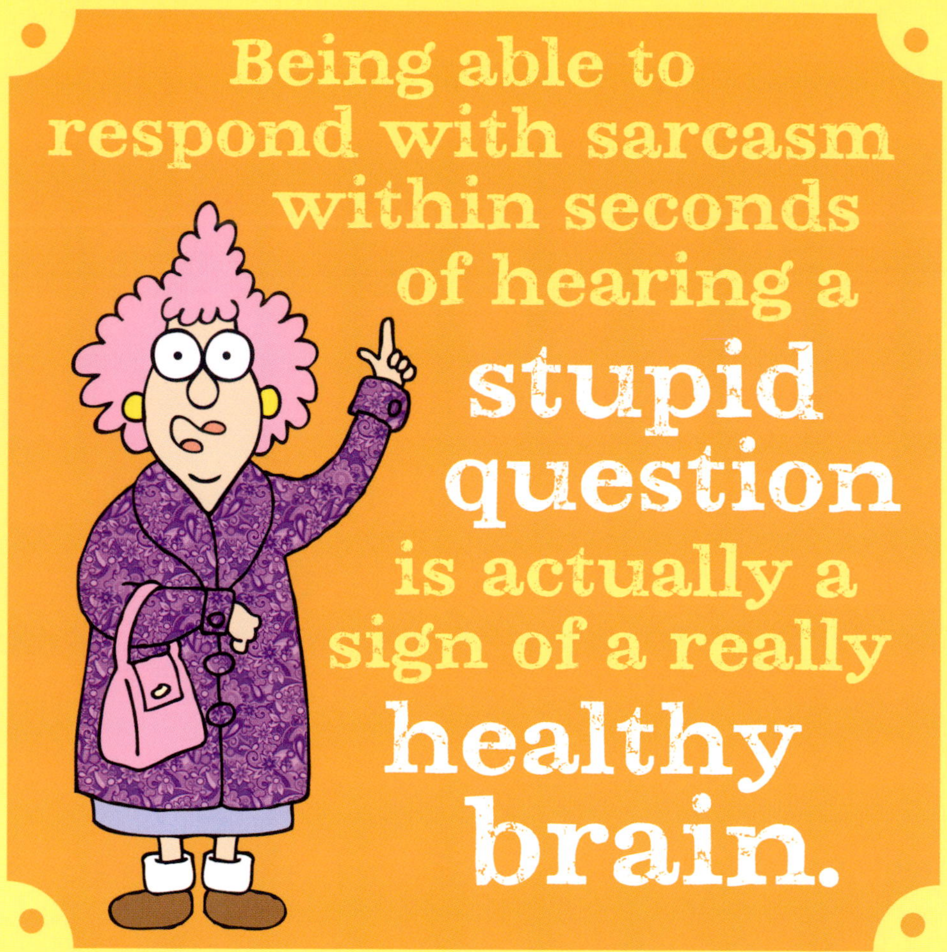

Being able to respond with sarcasm within seconds of hearing a **stupid question** is actually a sign of a really **healthy brain.**

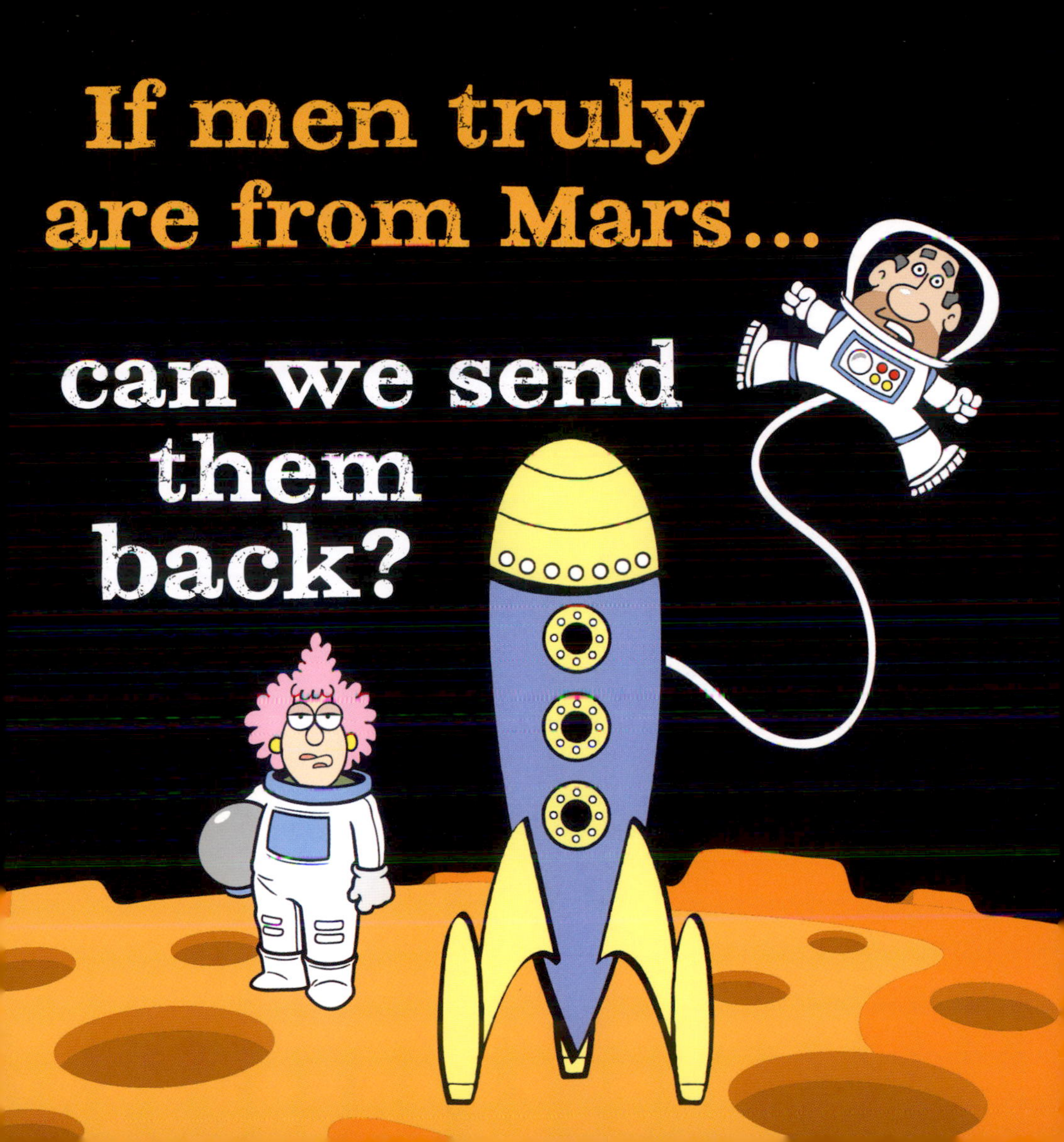
If men truly
are from Mars...
can we send
them
back?

aunty acid's

THOUGHTS FROM THE TUB

We say "hair" when referring to a lot of it, but "hairs" when referring to just a few.

Saying "I think outside the box" is using a tired, worn-out cliche to claim you are an original thinker.

How far back in history do you have to go before it becomes archaeology and not grave robbing?

If two people on opposite sides of the world drop a piece of bread, the earth briefly becomes a sandwich.

Milk is just immature cheese.

Most people's first word of the year is "Happy."

Getting a new set of teeth would be a lot more useful at age 60 than age 6.

FRIENDS & FAMILY

You don't have to be crazy to be my friend, but it helps...
Seriously, even if you have just ONE friend on your level of crazy, that one friend is all you will ever need. Luckily for me though, I have a whole bunch of nuts who I'm proud to be seen in public with (including you, dear reader)! The following pages contain some of my funniest gags on all things friendship, family and what being a GOOD buddy really means to me.

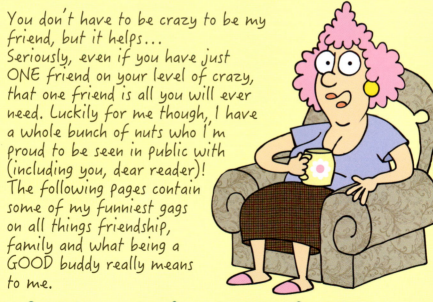

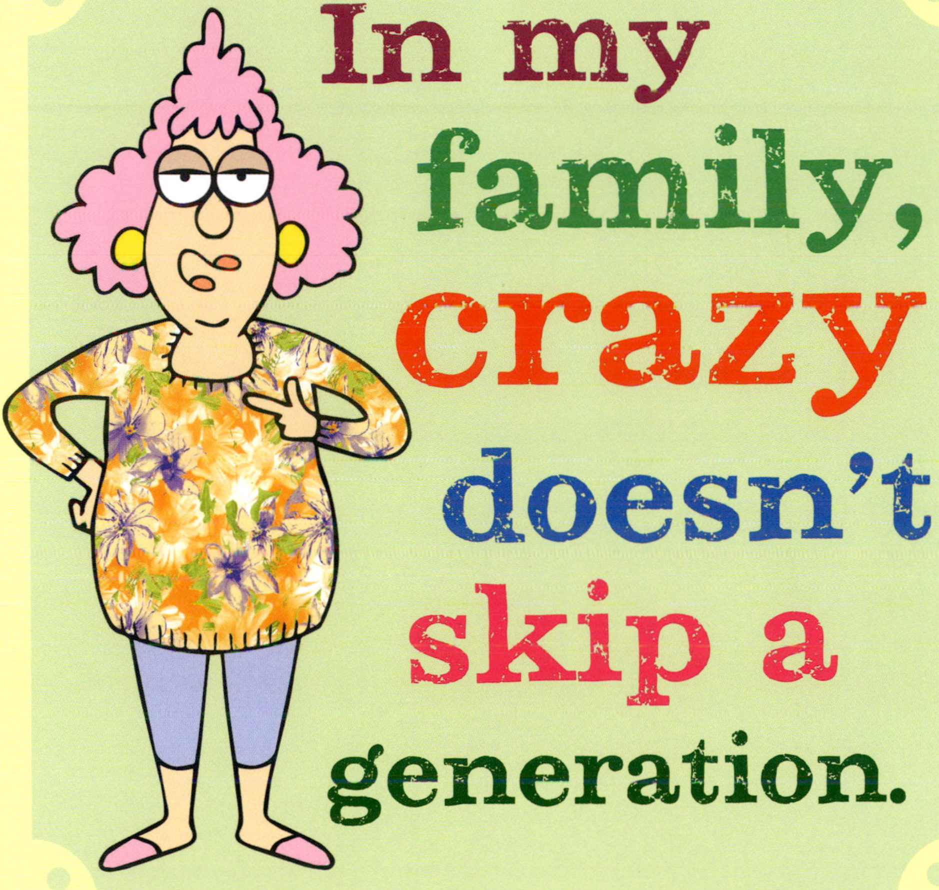

In my family, crazy doesn't skip a generation.

I can't remember if I'm the GOOD SISTER or the EVIL ONE.

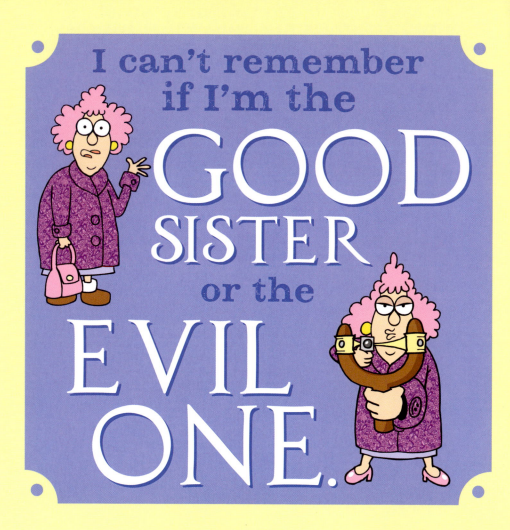

TO MY CHILDREN:
Never make fun of
having to help me with
computer stuff.

REMEMBER:
I taught you
how to use
a spoon!

Dear Mother-in-law,

I don't need your advice on how to raise my children.

I'm living with one of yours, and he needs a lot of improvement.

I know we're
good friends

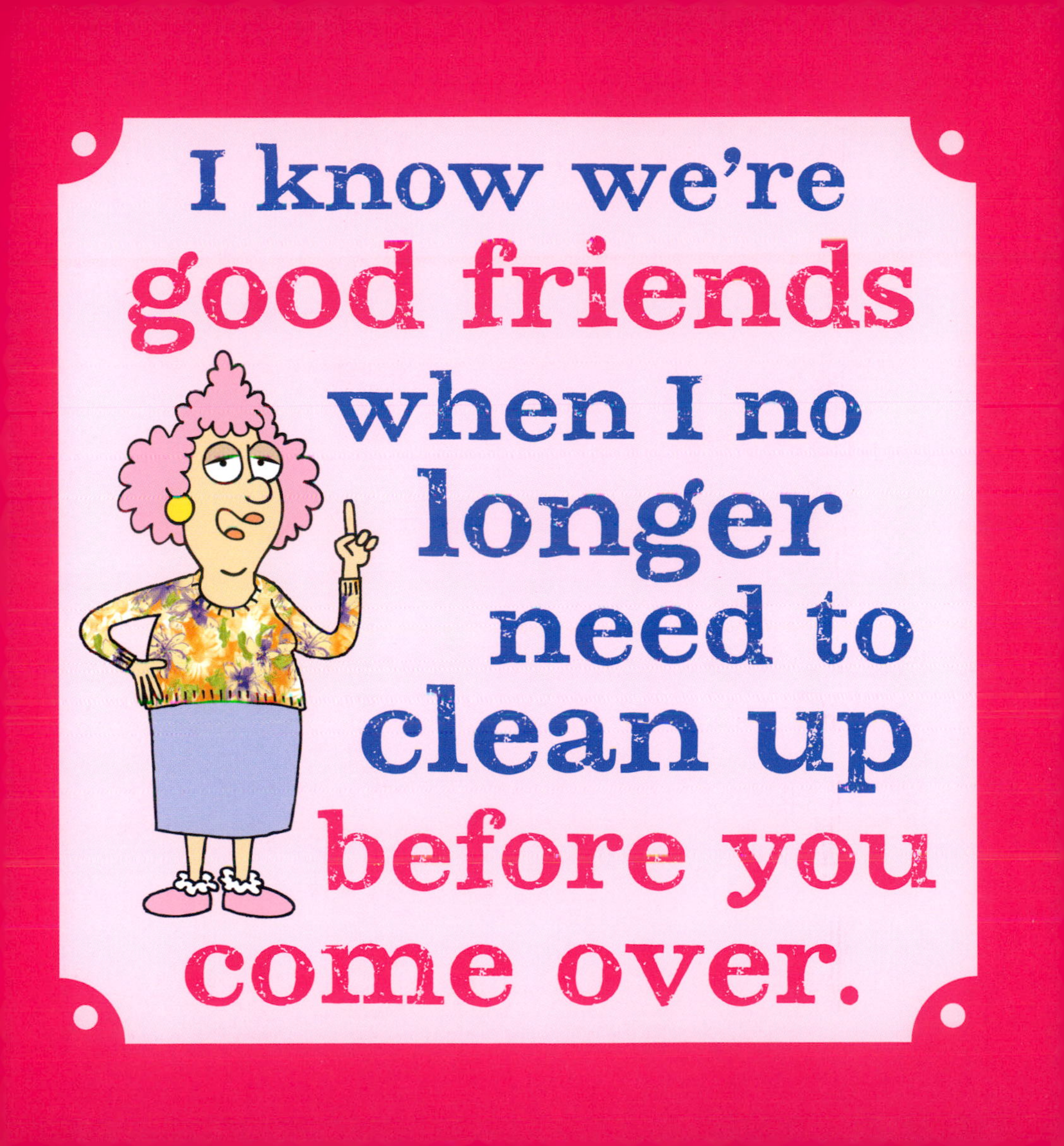

when I no
longer
need to
clean up
before you
come over.

We are
best friends.
Always remember
that if you
fall,

I will
pick you up...
after I finish
laughing.

OH CR*P!

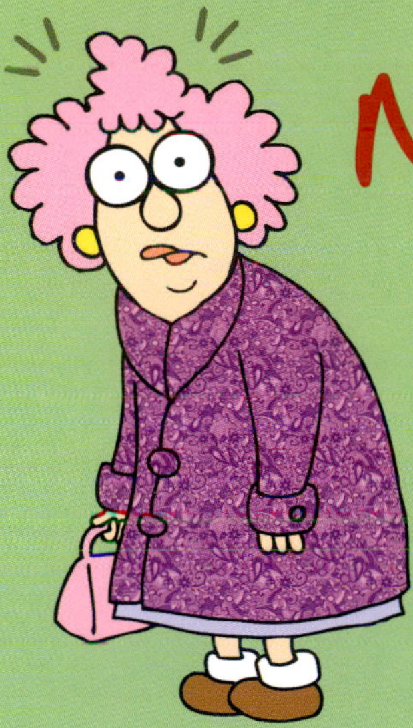

My Mother was right about everything!

Love and Romance

I've always said that love is like a toot; if you have to force it, it's probably cr*p. It should come naturally! Sure, love'll have its fair share of ups and downs, but there isn't a fun roller coaster that doesn't (although it shouldn't make you barf as much). All you need is a friend who matches your level of crazy and a partner you want to annoy for the rest of your freakin' life, and the rest falls into place. Don't look so shocked...I DO have a soft side. It's just waaay on the freakin' inside! So share a romantic bottle of champagne with yourself, and read on for some of my favorite laughs on all things love and romance.

No matter how serious life gets, you still gotta have that one person you can be completely stupid with.

It’s better to have
loved and lost
than to
spend the
rest of
your life
with a
dumbass.

Behind every
nagging woman,
there's a
man
not doing
what he's
supposed
to do!

The most romantic love story isn't **Romeo and Juliet** who died together.

It's **Grandpa** and **Grandma** who grew old together.

Being married is like having the **freedom** to do whatever **your wife** tells you.

Yes,
relationships
are great...
but have
you
ever
heard of
pizza?

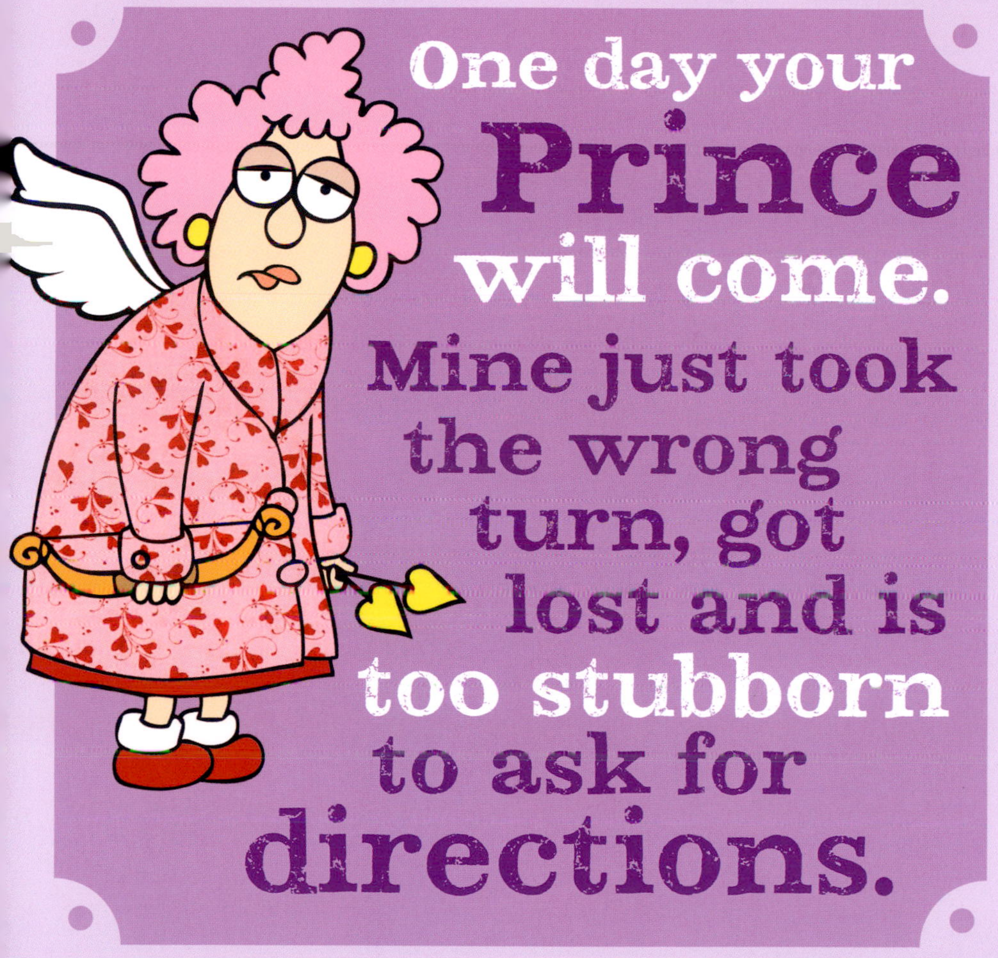

One day your **Prince** will come. Mine just took the wrong turn, got lost and is too stubborn to ask for **directions.**

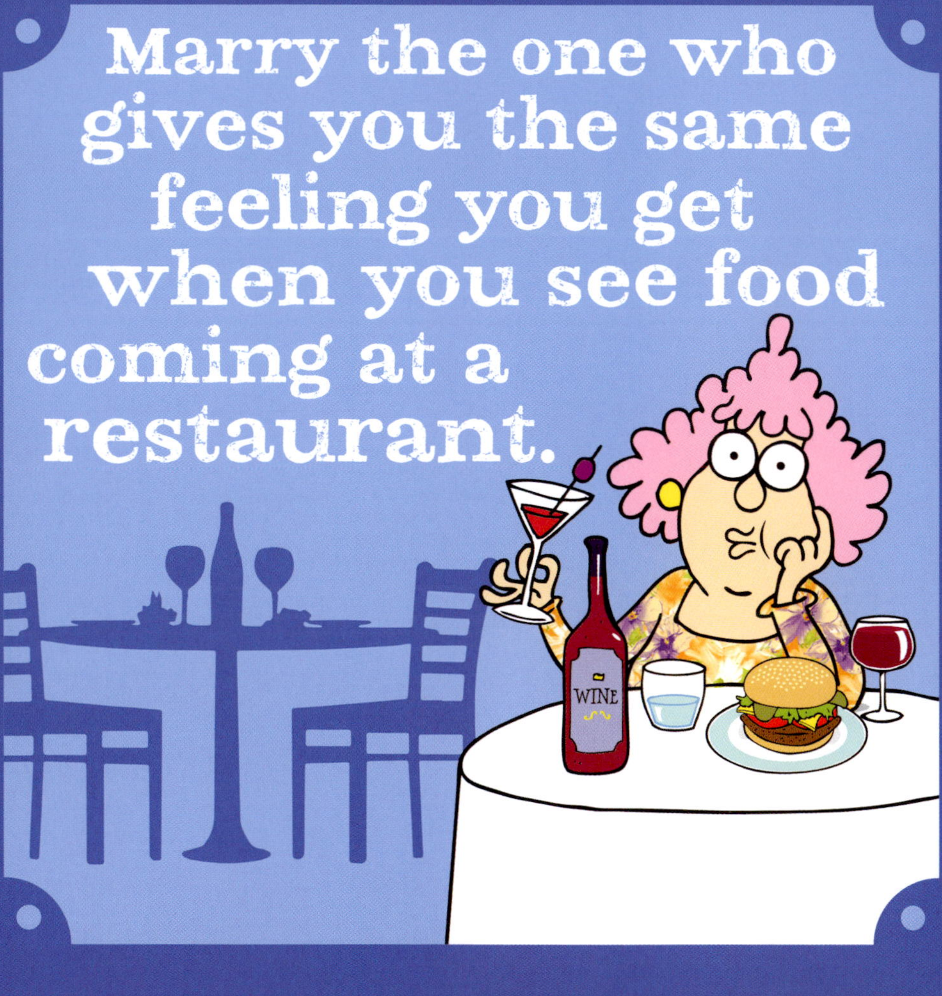
Marry the one who gives you the same feeling you get when you see food coming at a restaurant.
WINE

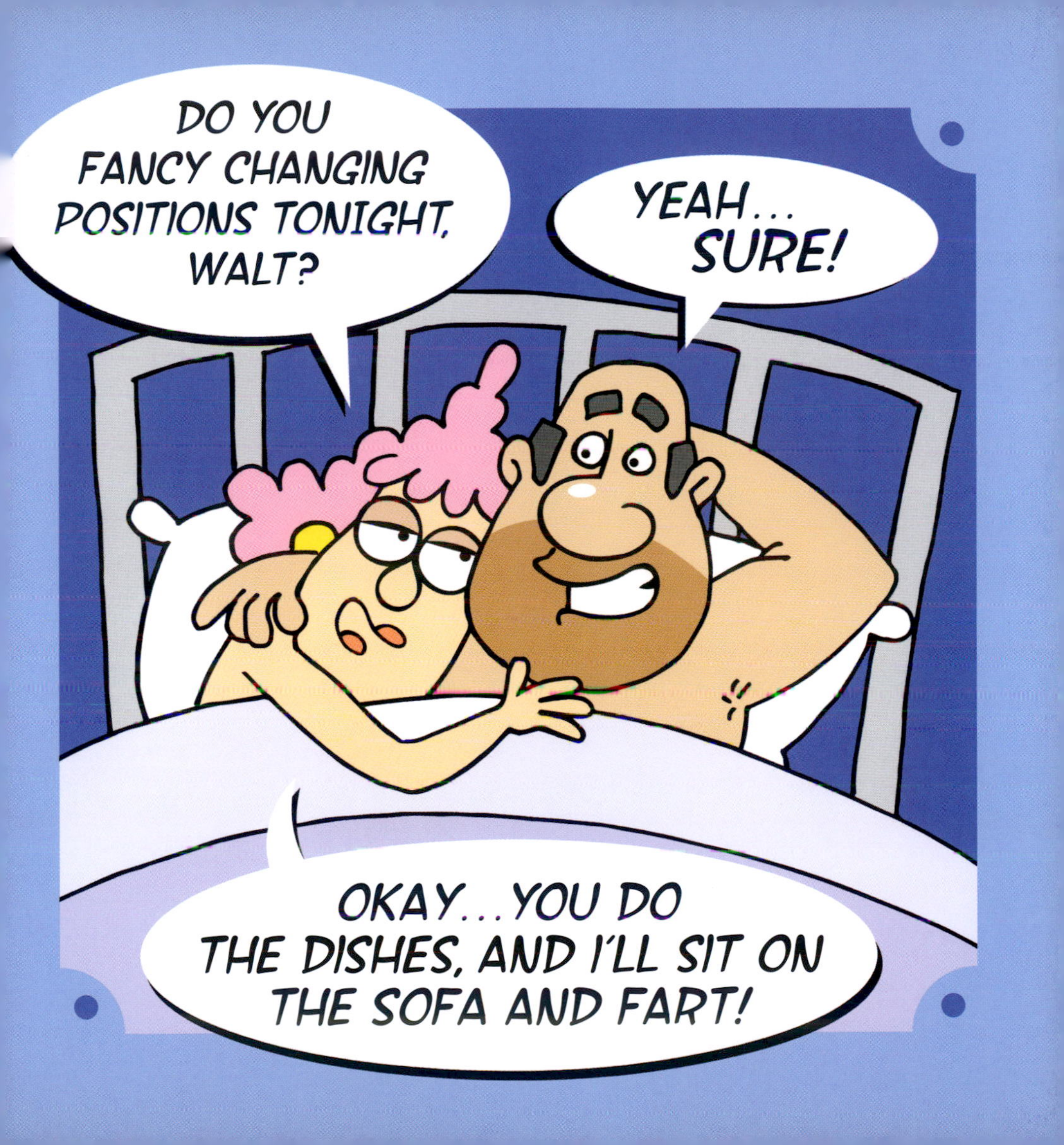
DO YOU FANCY CHANGING POSITIONS TONIGHT, WALT?
YEAH... SURE!
OKAY... YOU DO THE DISHES, AND I'LL SIT ON THE SOFA AND FART!

aunty acid's
THOUGHTS FROM THE TUB

Onion rings are vegetable donuts.

We will never hear about the truly perfect crime.

If your shirt isn't tucked into your pants, then your pants are tucked into your shirt.

Smoothies are just like cold fruit soup.

If I'm allergic to cats, I wonder if I'm allergic to lions?

If the oldest person on Earth is 116 years old, that means 117 years ago there was a completely different set of human beings on Earth.

I wonder what my dog named me?

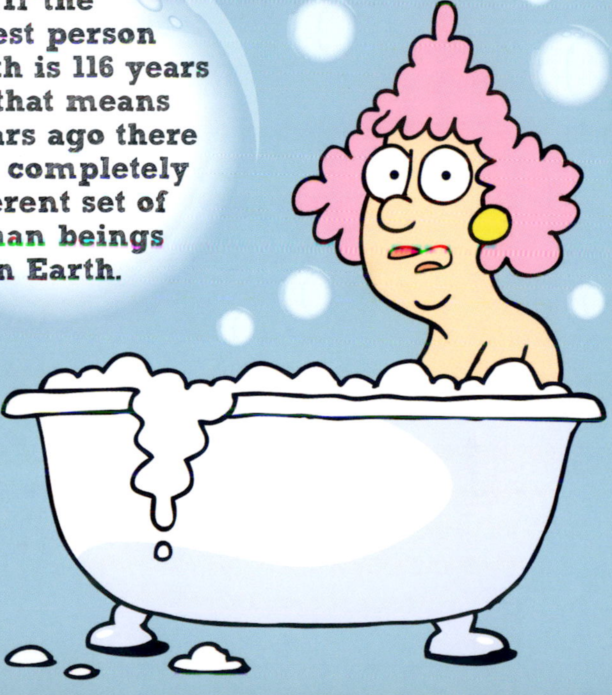

DIET AND EXERCISE

We all know that exercise and I are not exactly the best of friends. I just don't get how it's supposed to make you live longer when it makes me feel like I'm freakin' dying! Maybe with a bit more encouragement I'd do better? Once I thought I was being applauded on the treadmill until I realized it was just my butt cheeks clapping.

Now I've just vowed to stay away from anything that makes me look fat...such as scales, mirrors and photographs. So, my lovelies, don't sweat it! You're not alone in your gymophobia! Take a breather and read my best thoughts on EVIL diet and exercise!

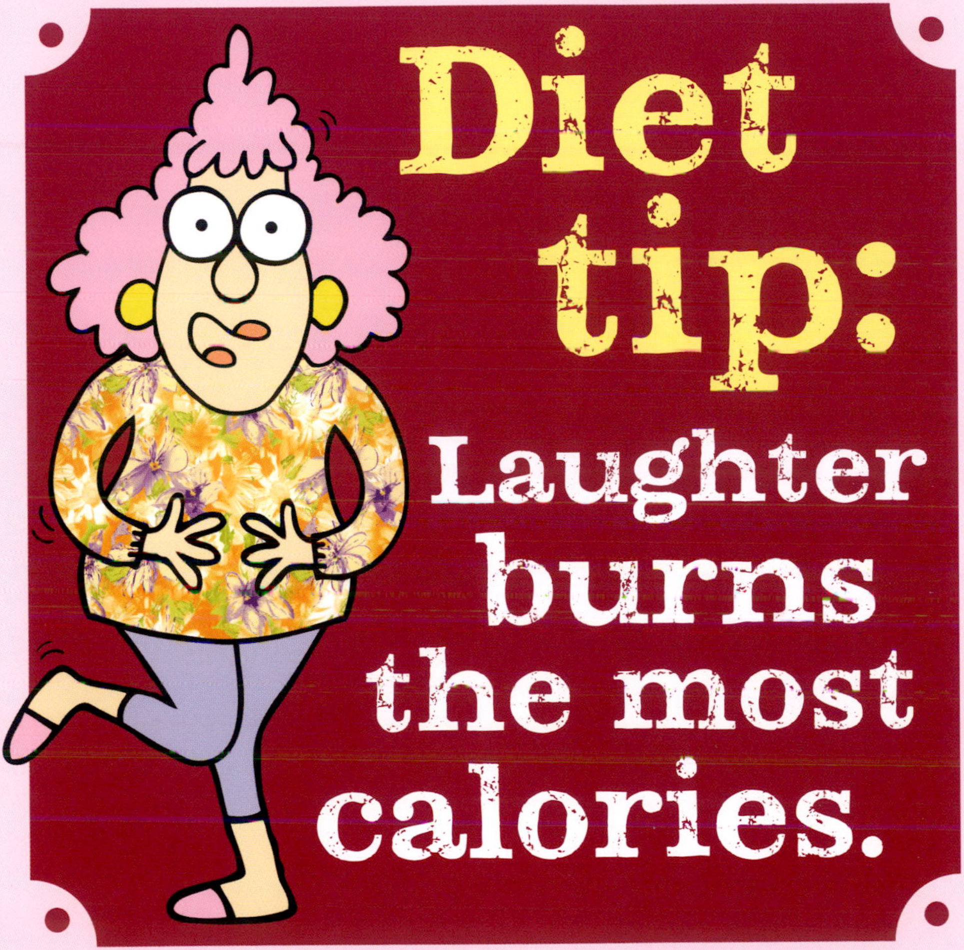
Diet tip:
Laughter burns the most calories.

EAT WHAT YOU WANT,

and if anyone tries to lecture you about your weight...

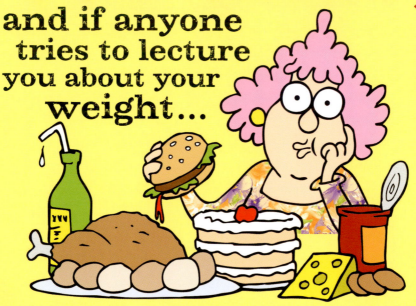

eat them too.

Fitness level:

Pulled a muscle in my ass just crossing my legs.

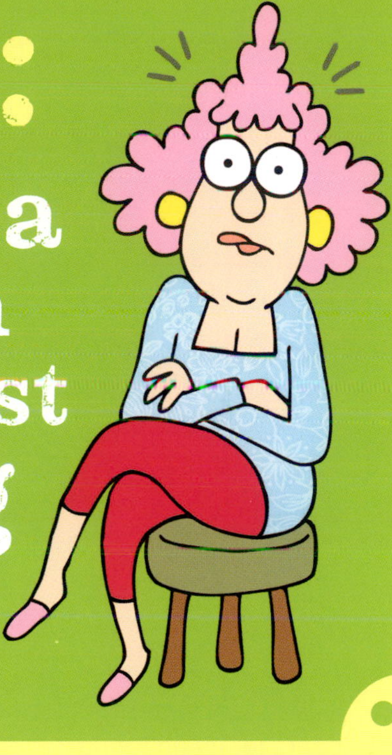

I have gotten out of bed **365 days a year for decades.**

That's over 17,000 sit-ups

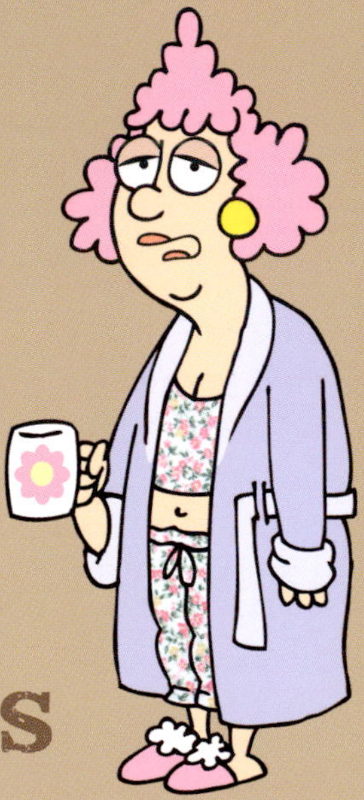

and not one ab to show for it!

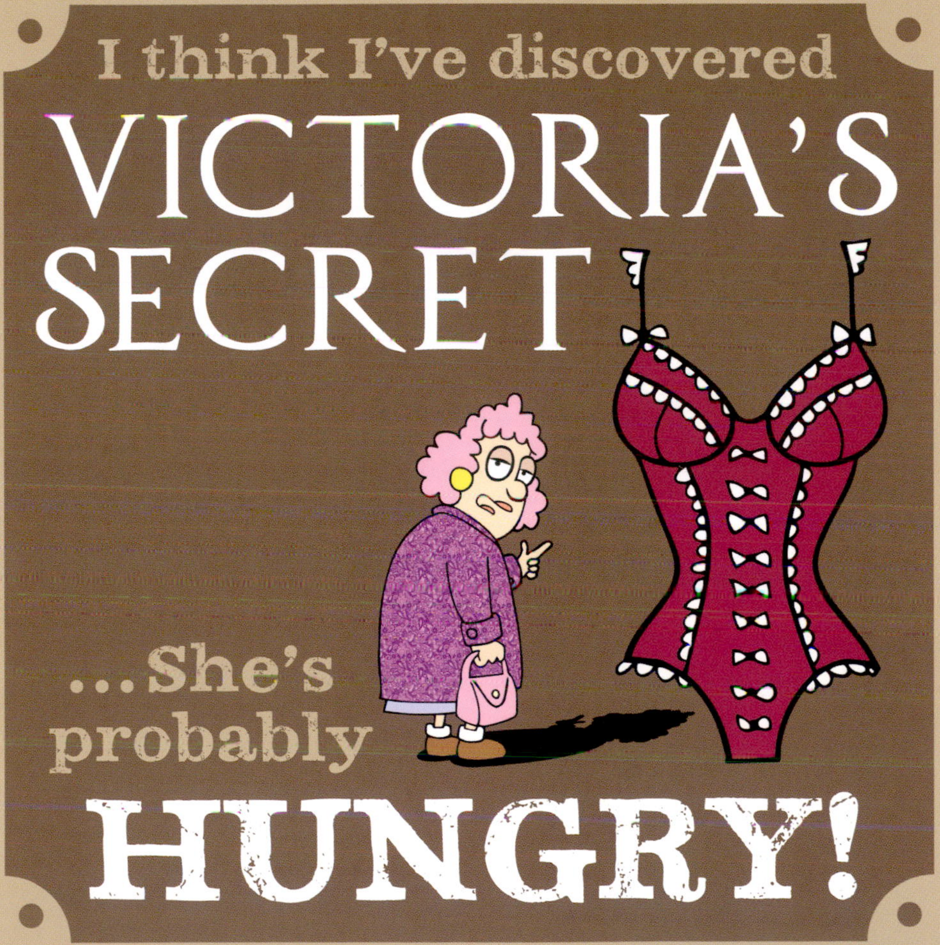
I think I've discovered
VICTORIA'S SECRET
...She's probably
HUNGRY!

I wish
I could
lose
weight
as easily as
I lose my
patience.

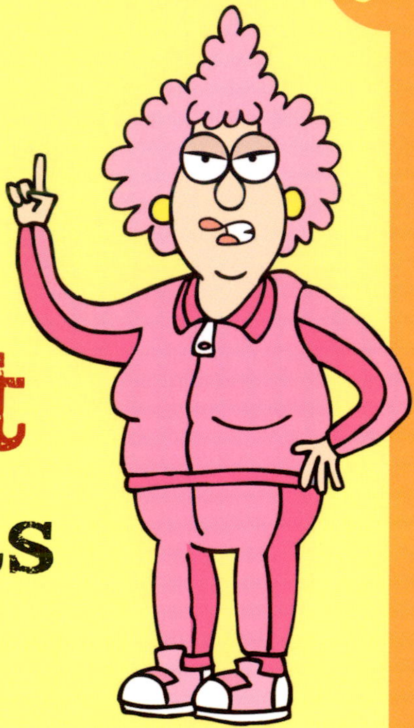

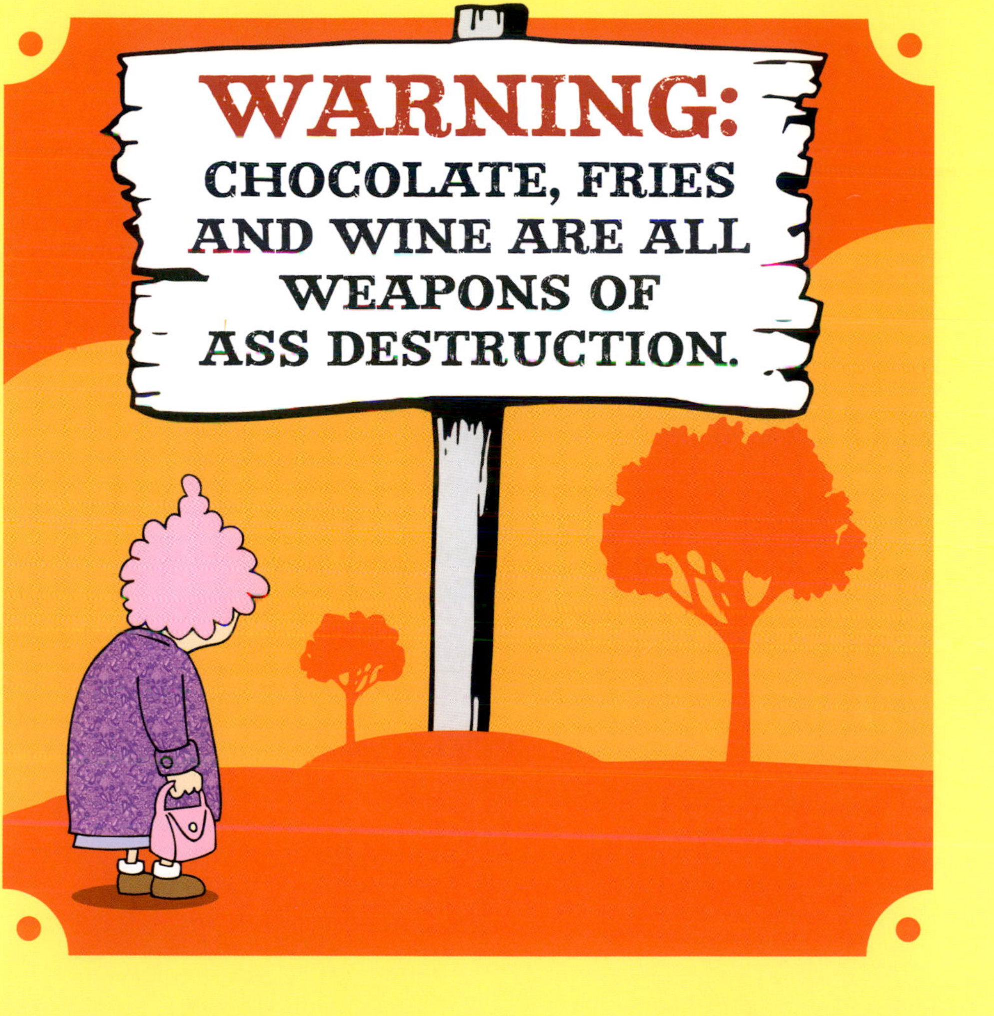
WARNING:
CHOCOLATE, FRIES
AND WINE ARE ALL
WEAPONS OF
ASS DESTRUCTION.

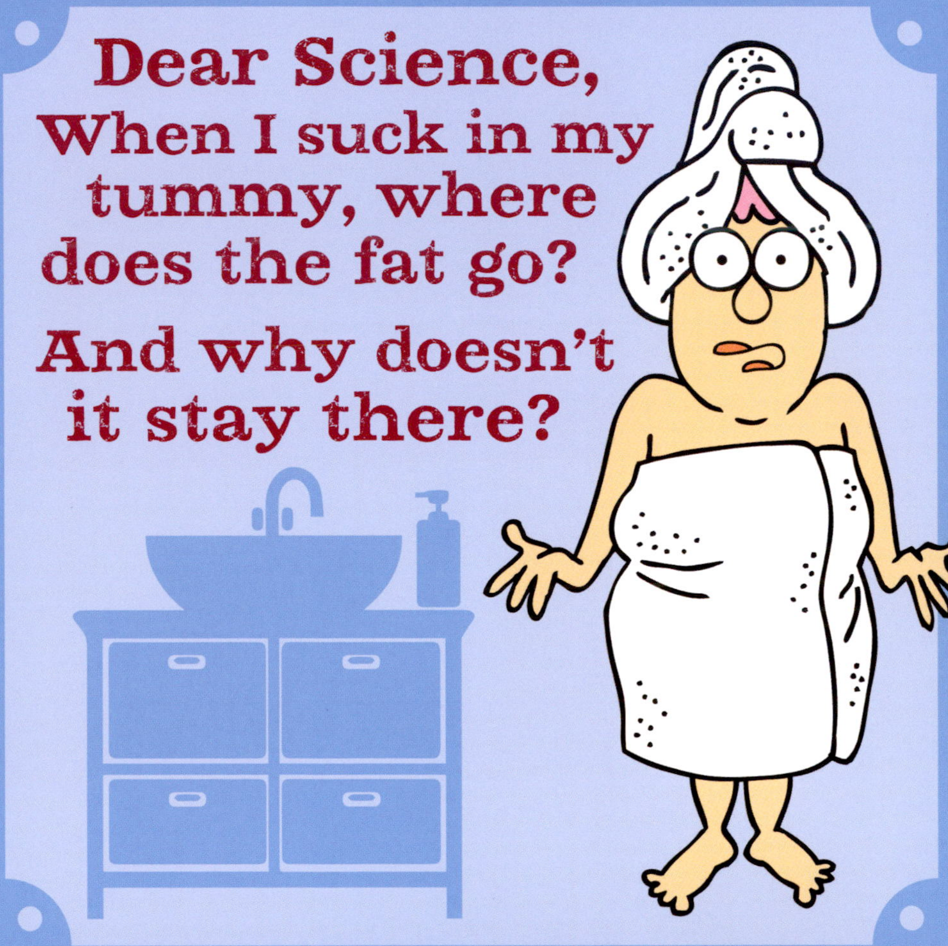
Dear Science,
When I suck in my tummy, where does the fat go?
And why doesn't it stay there?

Diet tip:

Your pants won't get too tight if you don't **wear any.**

AUNTY
ACID'S

DICTIONARY

I swear to tell the truth, the whole truth and...

well, anything that doesn't involve my freakin' age or weight!

I'm gonna tell you some home truths about the REAL meaning of words. Those dictionary guys think they're the ones with all the brain sauce? Well, let me freakin' tell you that until you've walked a mile in my slippers, you might want to read on and learn some stuff they were too afraid to teach you in school!

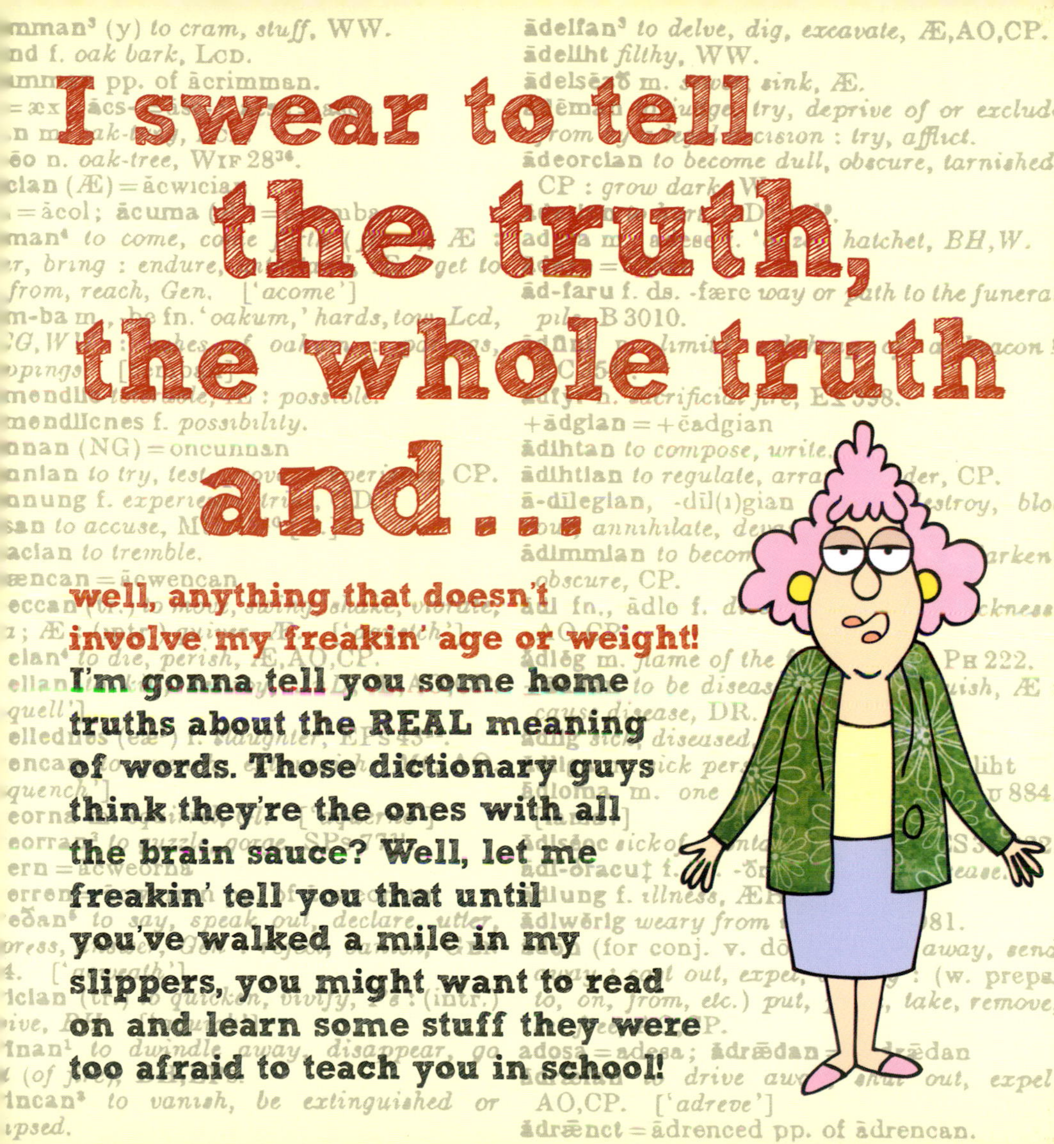

Nutella (proper noun)
The only reason to buy bread.

Secret (noun)
Something you tell everybody to tell nobody.

Argument (noun)
A discussion that occurs when you're right—and continues until they realize it.

Vegan (noun)
A mass murderer of thousands of innocent fruits and vegetables.

Calories (noun)
Tiny creatures that live in your closet and sew your clothes a little bit tighter every night.

Nillionaire (noun)
Someone having little or no money.

Feet (noun)
A device used for finding Legos in the dark.

Askhole (noun)
A person who constantly asks for your advice but always does the opposite of what you tell them.

Single (adjective)
A man who makes jokes about women in the kitchen.

Shower (noun)
An alternative term for "Personal Concert Hall."

Drunk (adjective)
When you feel sophisticated but can't pronounce it.

Blonde jokes (noun)
Jokes short enough for men to understand.

K (phrase)
This conversation is now over.

Optimist (noun)
Someone who figures that taking a step backwards after taking a step forward is not a disaster, it's more like a cha-cha.

Pets (noun)
The only members of your family you actually like.

Mother (noun)
One person who does the work of twenty. For free.

Poor (adj)
When you have too much month at the end of your money.

Synonym (noun)
A word used in place of one you can't spell.

Never mind (phrase)
You were too stupid to understand it the first time, so I give up trying to explain it.

Laziness (adjective)
The willingness to risk dropping everything you carry rather than making two trips.

Tomorrow (noun)
A mythical land where 99% of all human activity, motivation and achievement is stored.

Friend (noun)
One of the many strangers on Facebook.

Democracy (noun)
The freedom to elect our own dictators.

I'll pay you back (phrase)
You'll never see this money again.

aunty acid's
THOUGHTS FROM THE TUB

In a 500-day period, I could meet someone, get married, have a baby and get divorced—and yet I'd still be using the same box of Q-tips.

If a cyclops has one eye, would he wink or blink?

Is an orange called an orange because it's orange...or is the color orange called orange because of an orange?

If a redhead goes crazy, is it called "Ginger Snaps"?

Most people are buried in suits and dresses, so a zombie apocalypse would be a formal event.

The first person to say the word "cool" must have been really cool, because everyone started saying it.

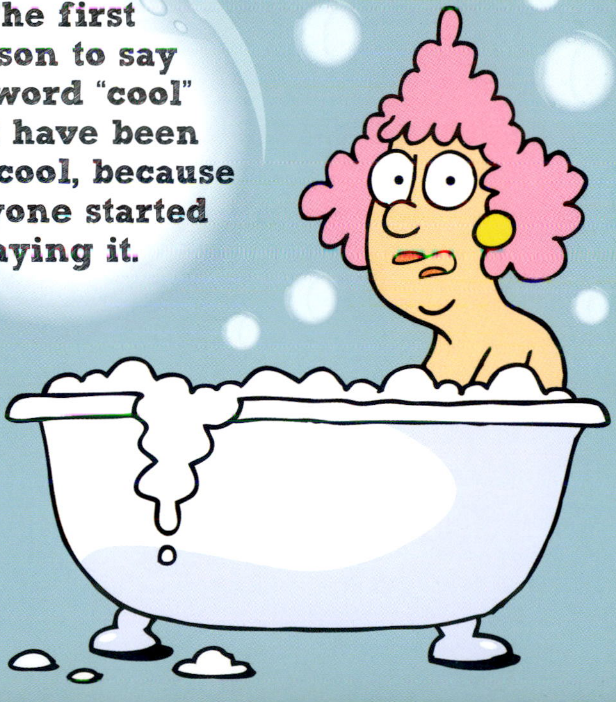

Would a Transformer get life insurance or car insurance?

Food & Drink

My life was once a constant struggle between wanting food and not wanting to get fat. These days...not so much! After years of fighting fries and cardio warfare, the battle has been won—the fries stand victorious. I have finally given up trying to be thin and opted for being just freakin' sexy instead! So please, help yourself and binge upon my many best bits, all about FOOD & DRINK. I hope this section gets you feeling those same love butterflies I get at the sight of a fudge cake or the sniff of three-cheese, stuffed-crust, deep-pan pizza.

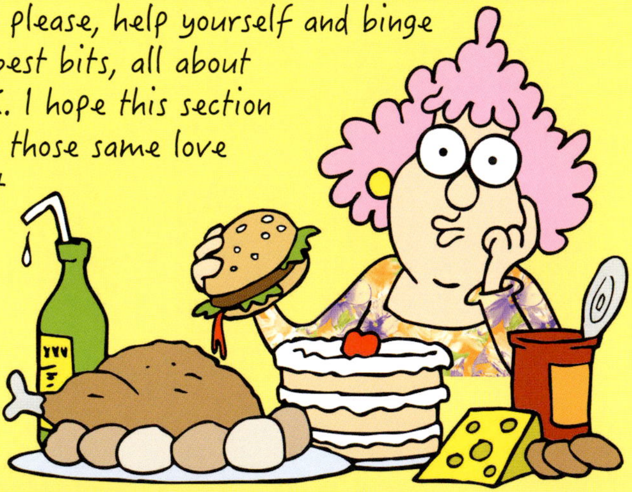

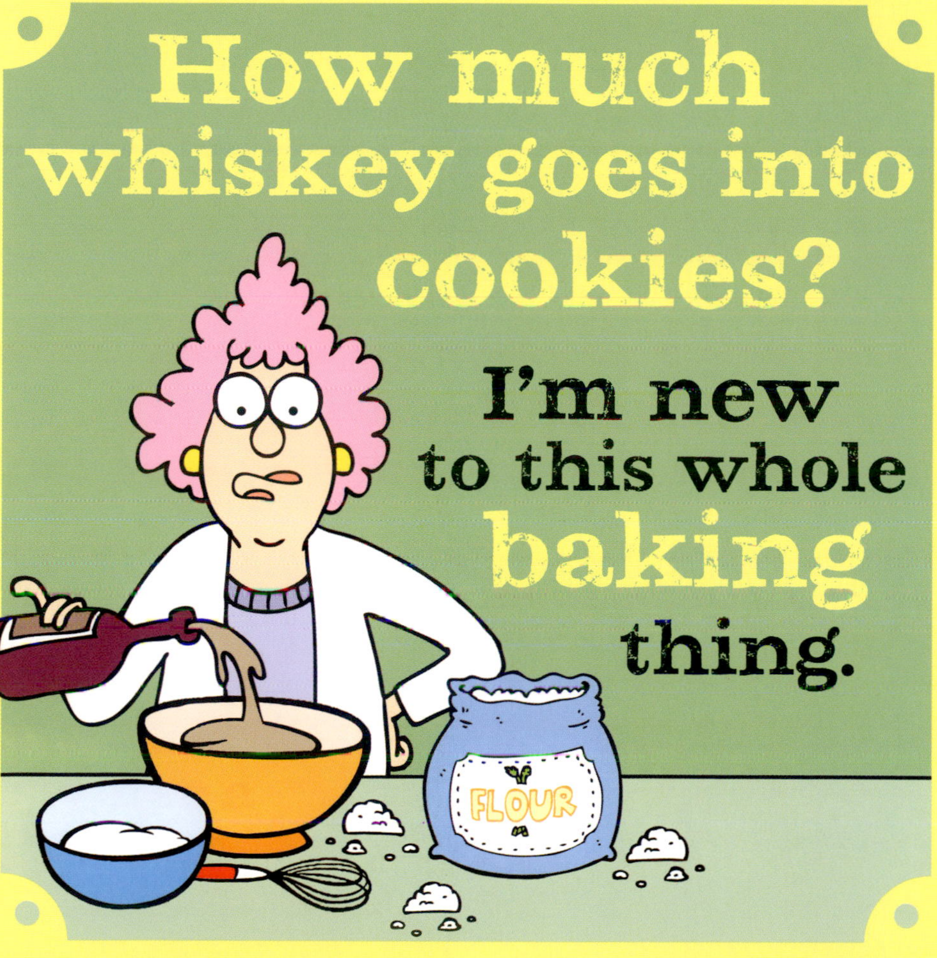
How much whiskey goes into cookies?
I'm new to this whole baking thing.
FLOUR

Welcome to Karma Café.

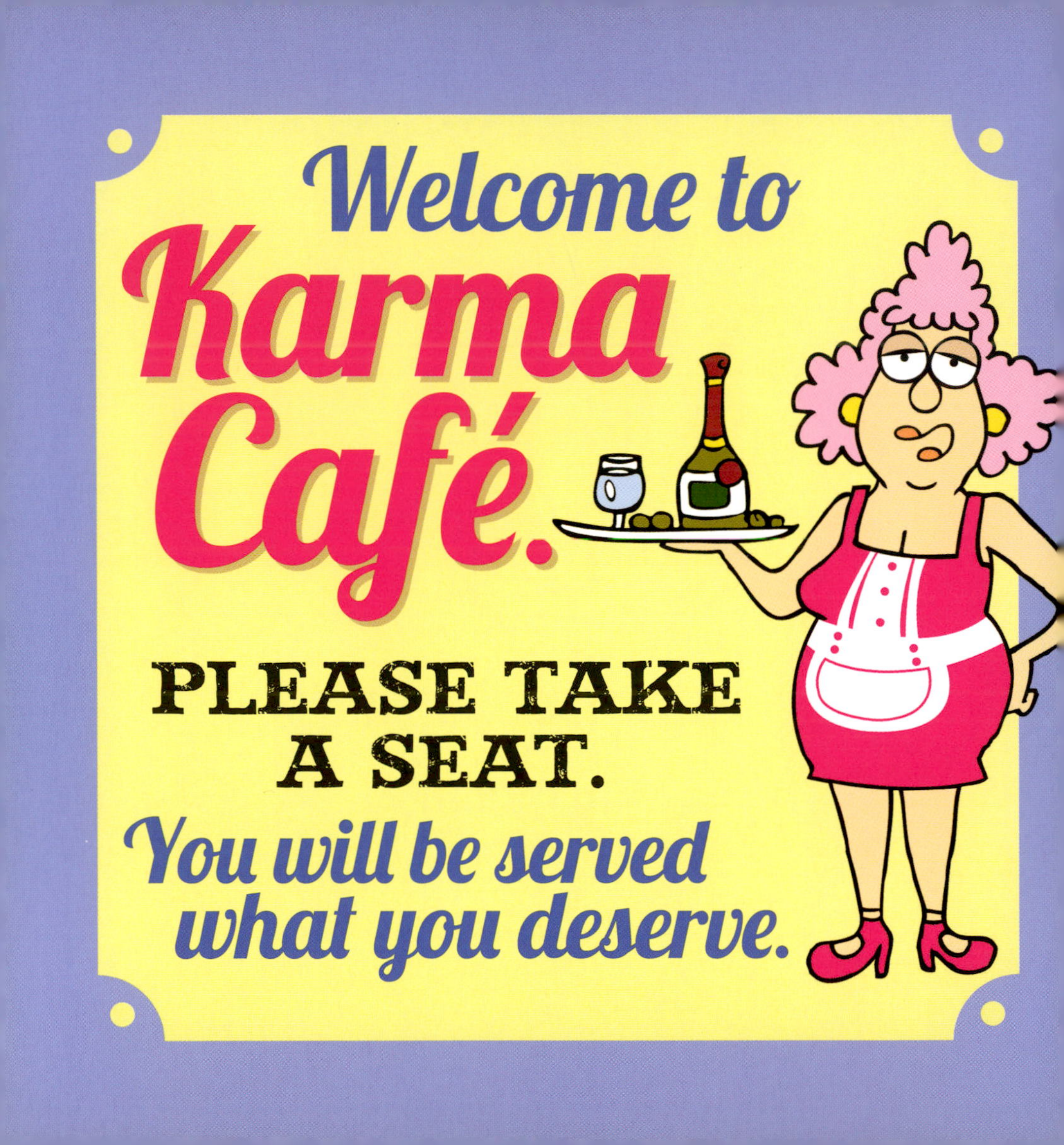

PLEASE TAKE A SEAT.

You will be served what you deserve.

You are what you eat? Well, I'd rather be a cupcake than a freakin' carrot anyway!

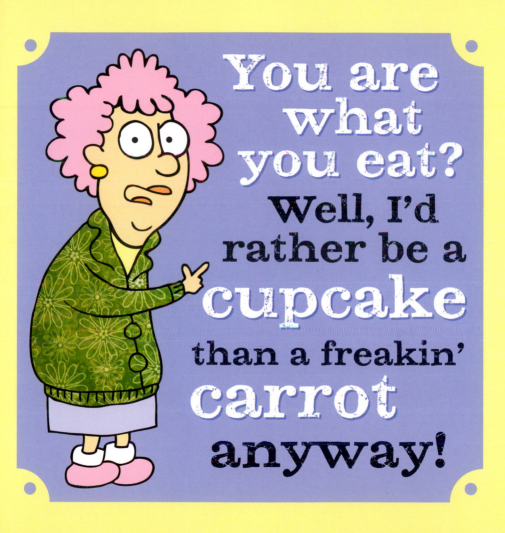

I'd rather eat
crumbs
with
bums
than eat
steaks
with
snakes.

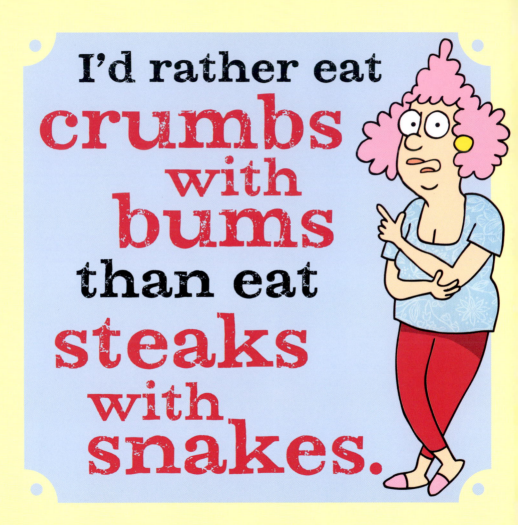

Fairy tales don't exist?

Hey, I drink a potion made from *magic beans* **every day that stops me from going crazy.** It's called **COFFEE.**

Caffeine
is bad for you.
Fat
is bad for you.
Sugar
is bad for you.
BUT DON'T
WORRY...
Worrying
is bad for
you too.

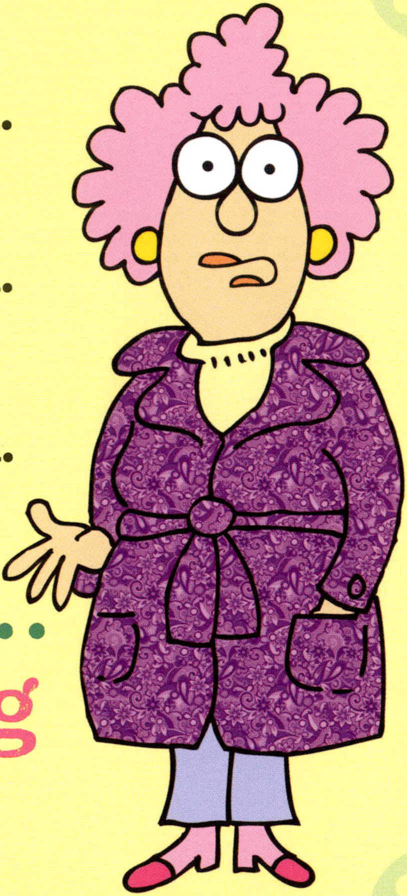

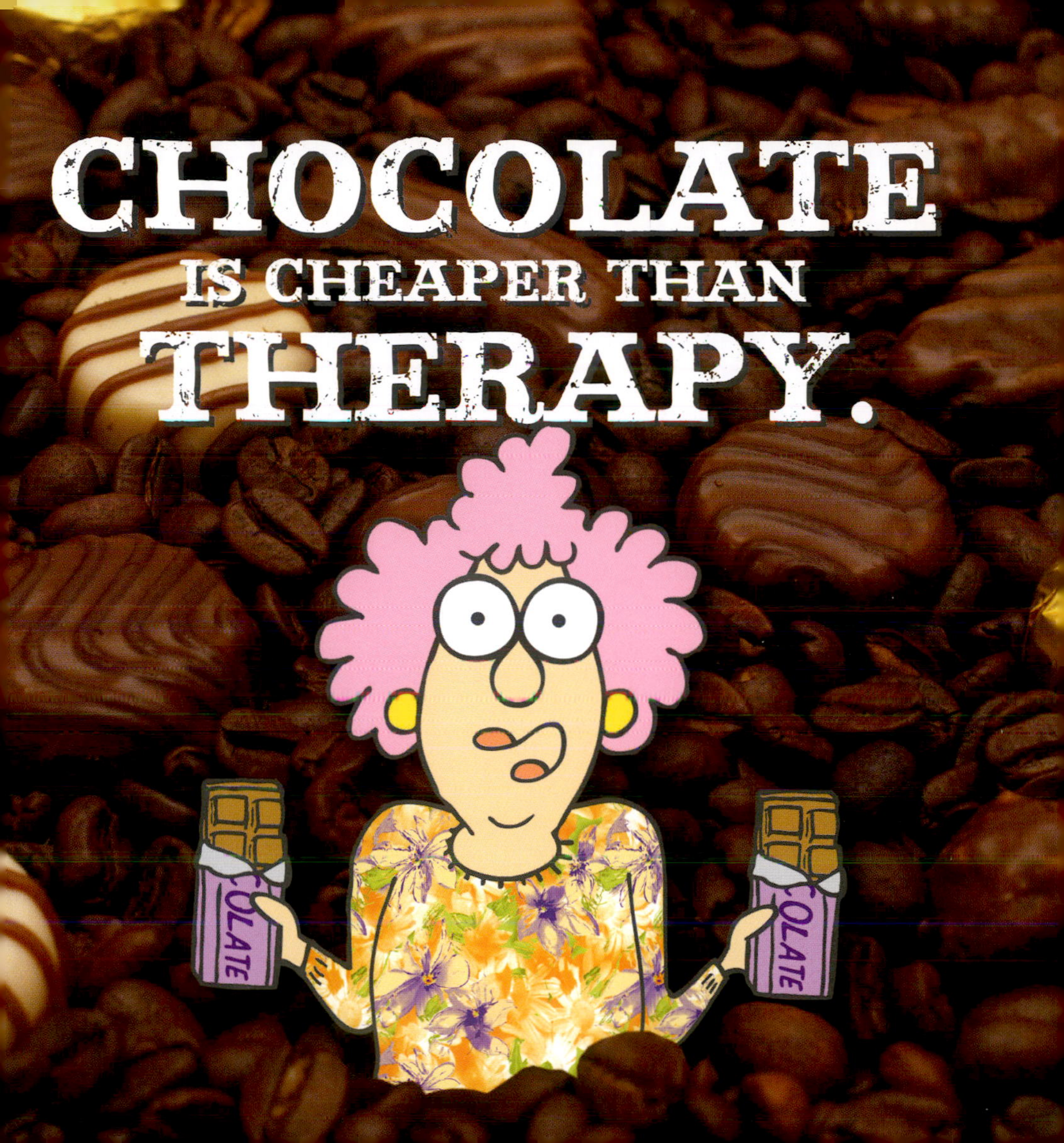
CHOCOLATE
IS CHEAPER THAN
THERAPY.

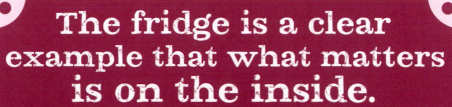

The fridge is a clear example that what matters is on the inside.

It's hard to

lose weight

when you

have an

over-

active

knife

& fork.

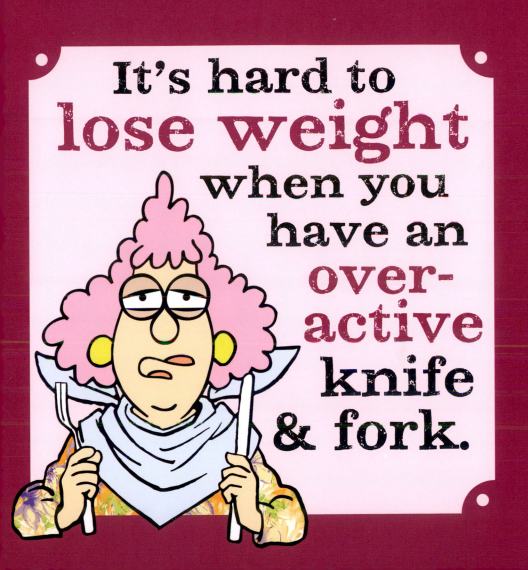

THOUGHTS FROM THE TUB

Doors are just really short tunnels.

I wonder how all of the signatures of people with the same name as me look.

Thanks to the word "indescribable," there's nothing that cannot be described.

Bad handwriting is like mumbling on paper.

If I use my vacuum, it collects dust. If I DON'T use my vacuum, it collects dust.

At a top speed of 27.78 mph, it is illegal for Usain Bolt to run in a school zone.

My car keys have more mileage than my car.

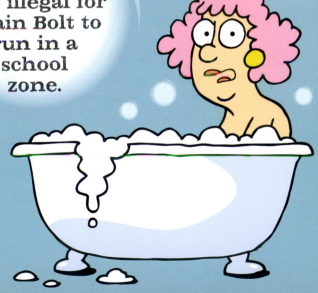

Getting Older...

DEAR LIFE,

I have decided this being an adult thing is too freakin' hard. If you need me, I'll be in my coloring fort eating Froot Loops. Thank you for the opportunity, but umm...

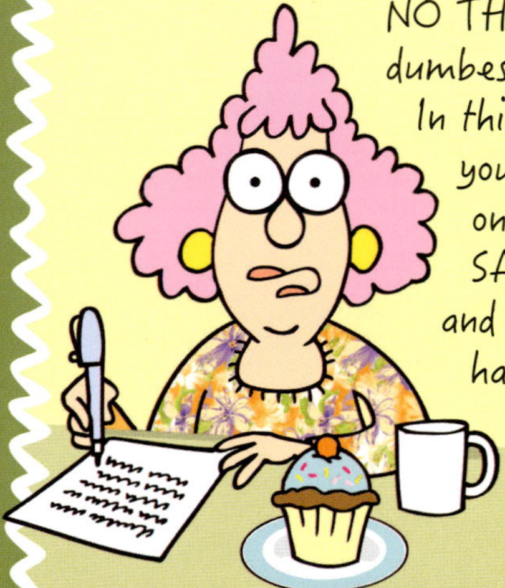

NO THANK YOU. Seriously, growing up is the dumbest thing I've ever done; how about you? In this section, my fair-weather friends, you'll find all my moaning and musings on everything AGE related, including SAGGING BOOBS, GETTING CRANKY, and the golden age of growing up without having your nose surgically attached to a screen. Remember when social networking meant actually playing OUTSIDE?! Enjoy!

The trouble with **Mondays** is I have to **adult.** I don't want to **adult.**

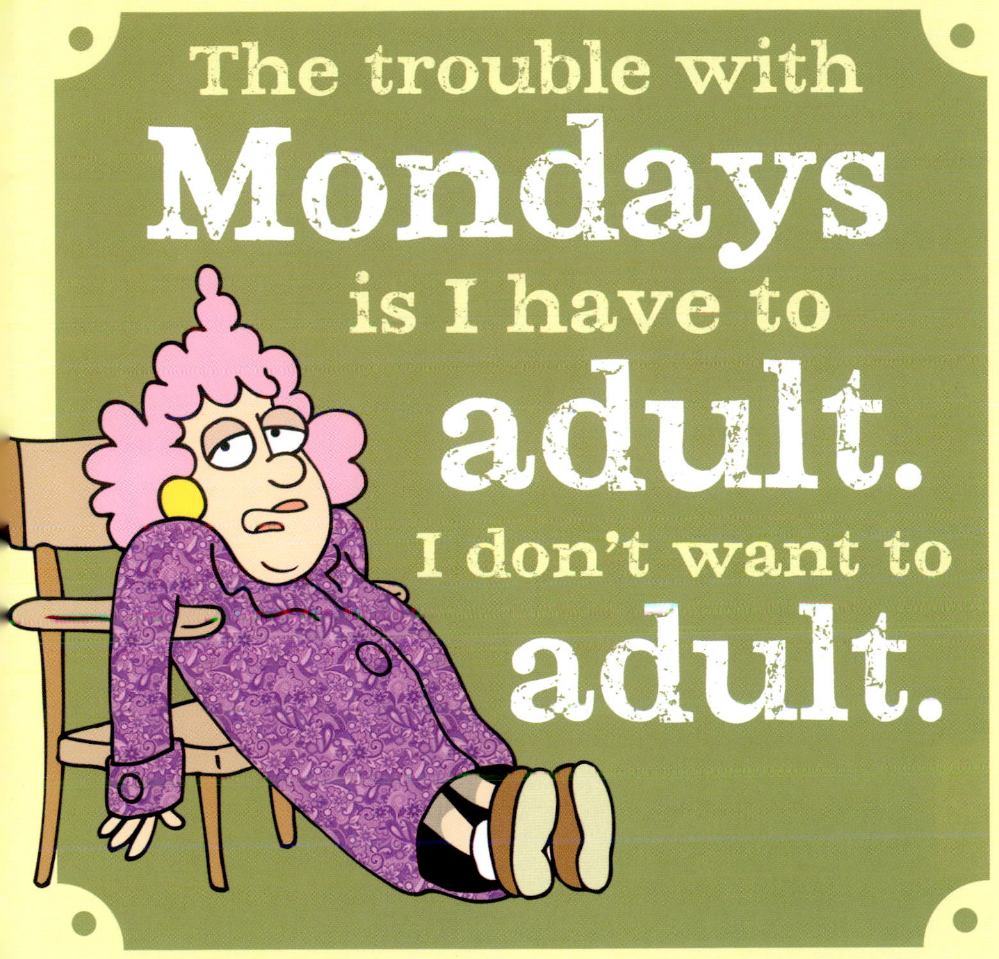

Don't stress about
your eyesight failing
as you age...

IT'S JUST
NATURE'S WAY
OF PROTECTING YOU
FROM GETTING A SHOCK
WHEN YOU WALK PAST A MIRROR.

Reach for the

STARS.

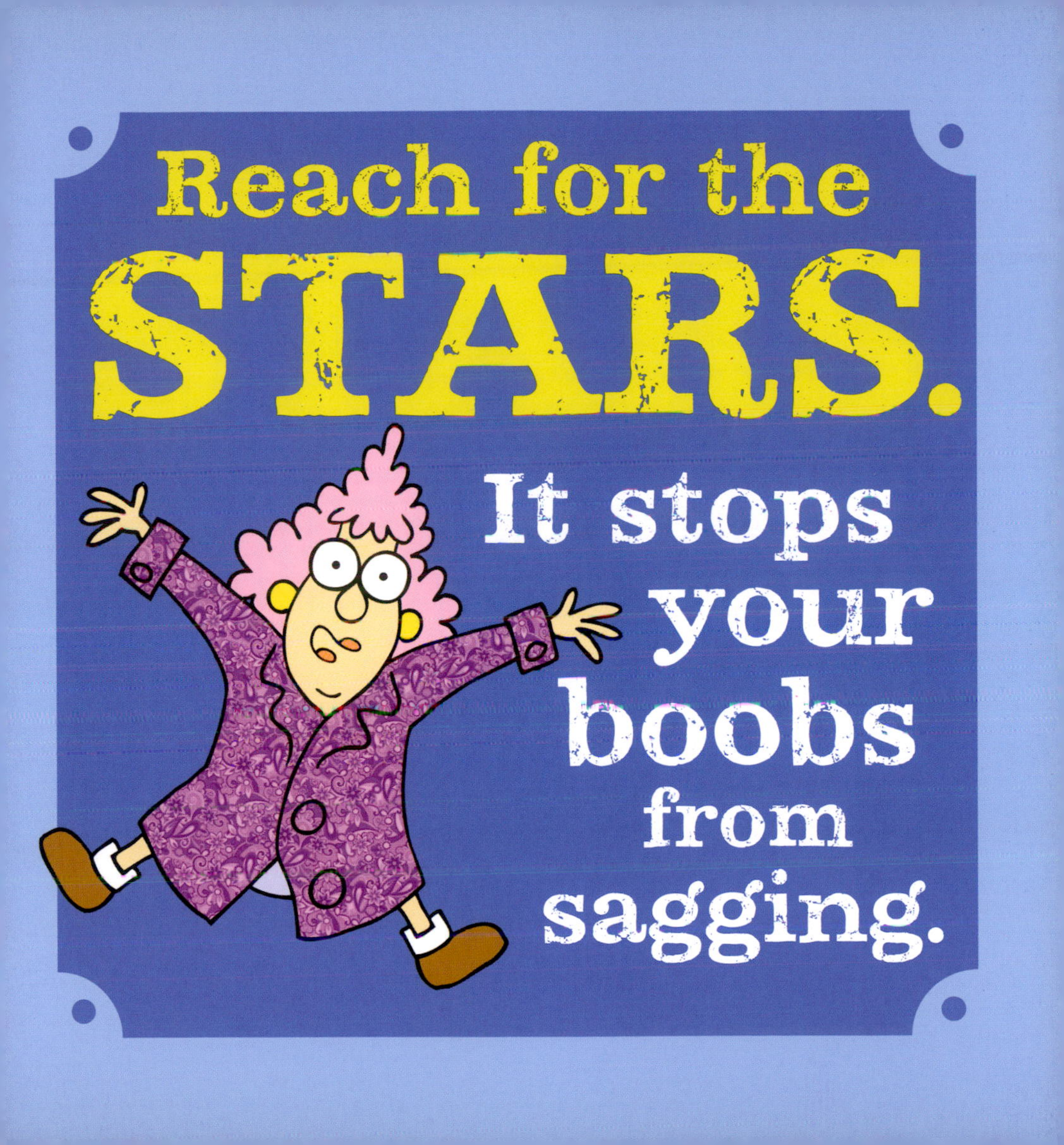

It stops your boobs from sagging.

When I was young, **$20** felt like **$100.** Now $20 feels like $1.

My morning routine includes: 10 minutes sitting in bed and thinking about how tired I am.

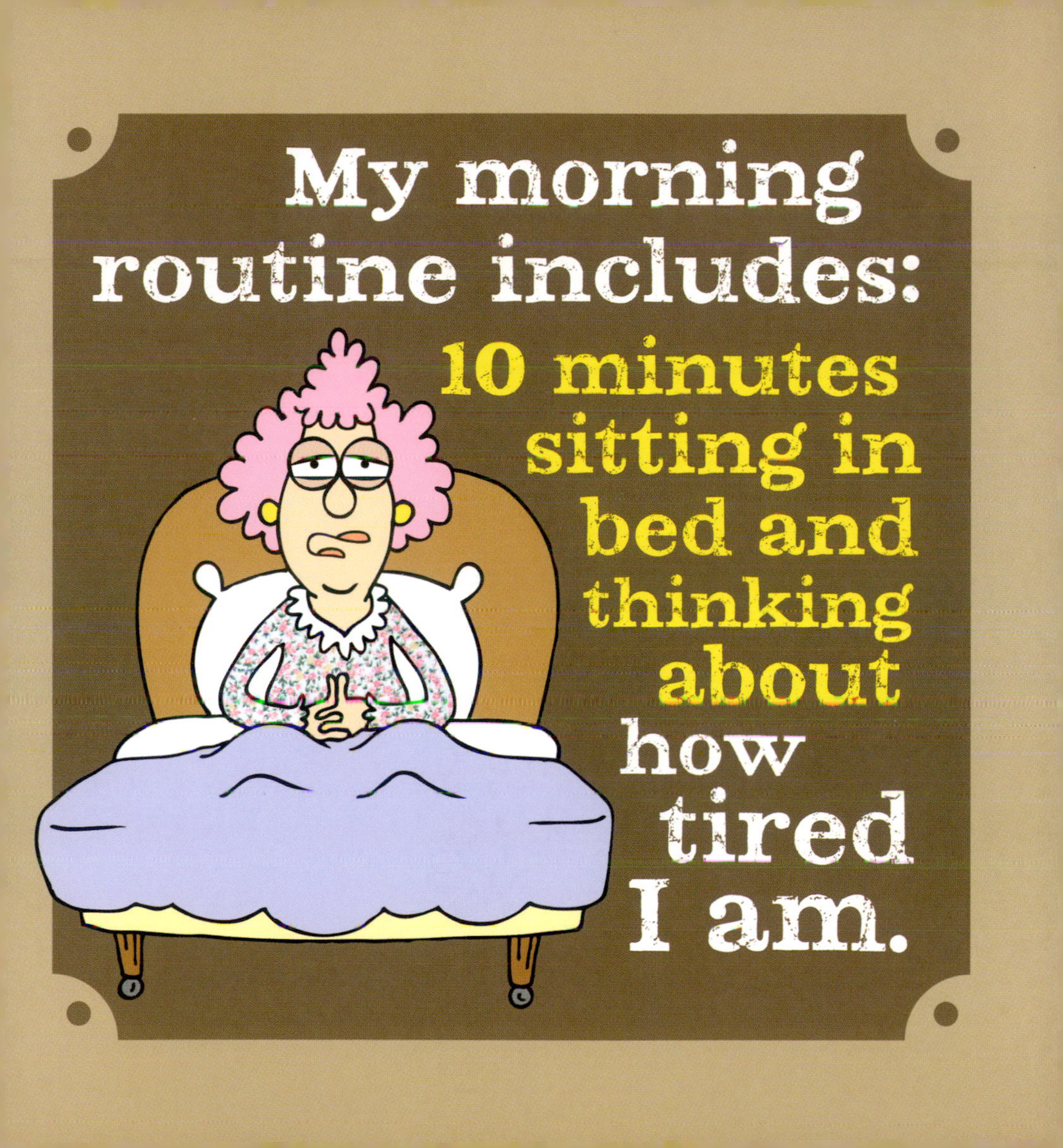

What's my favorite childhood memory?

Not paying bills.

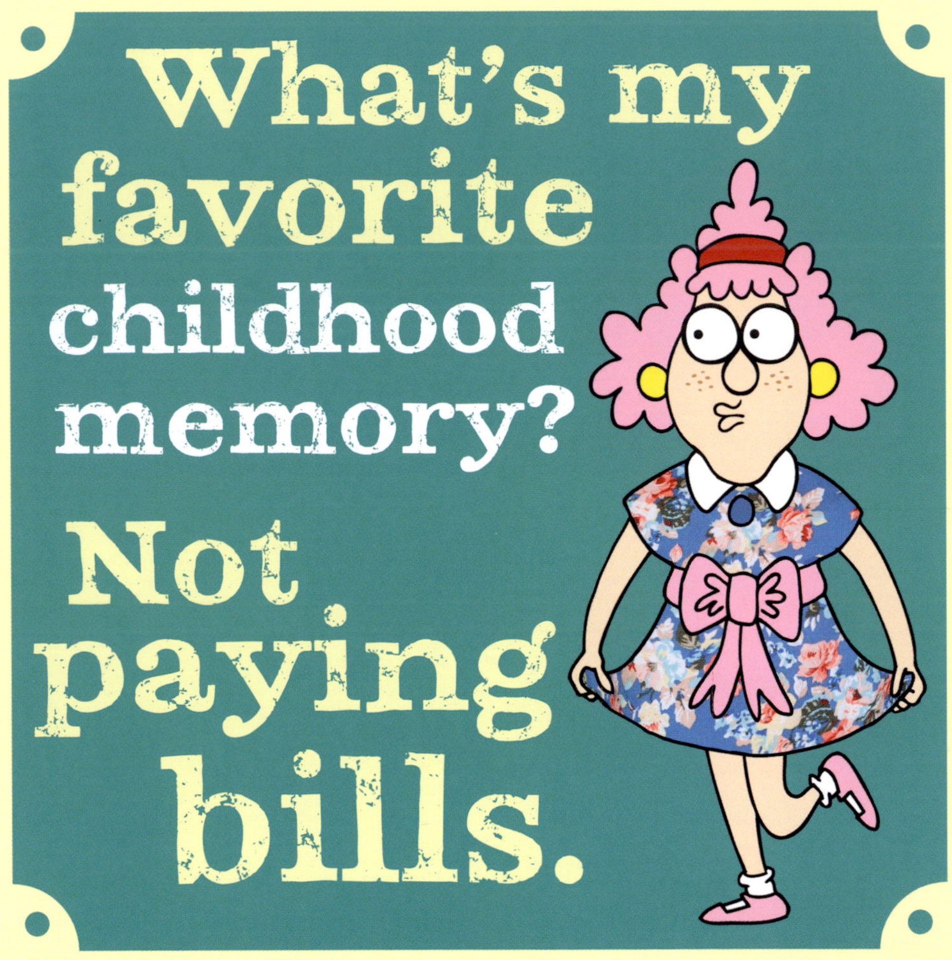

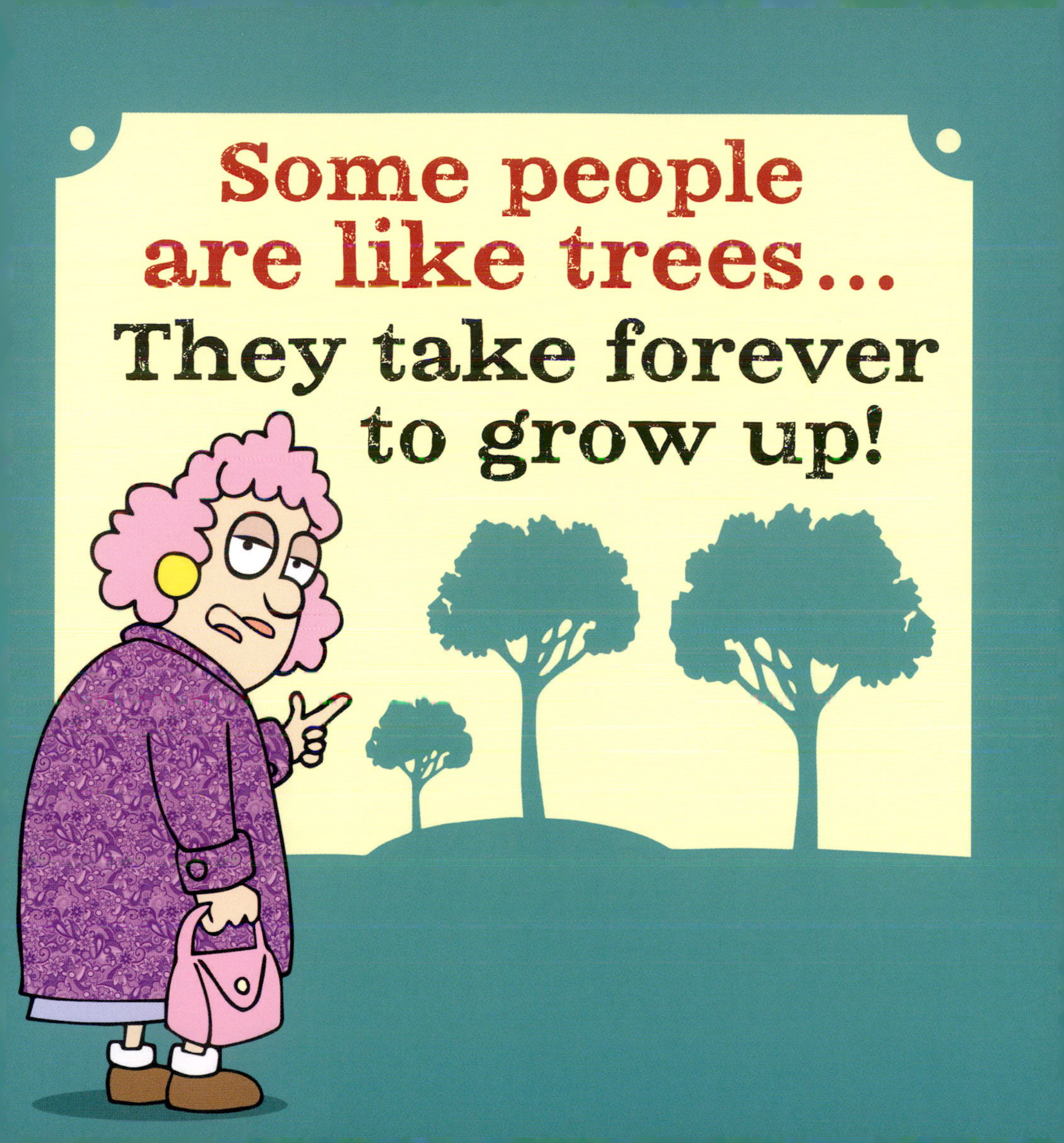
Some people are like trees...
They take forever to grow up!

When I say
“I’M BROKE,”
it doesn’t mean
I have $0.

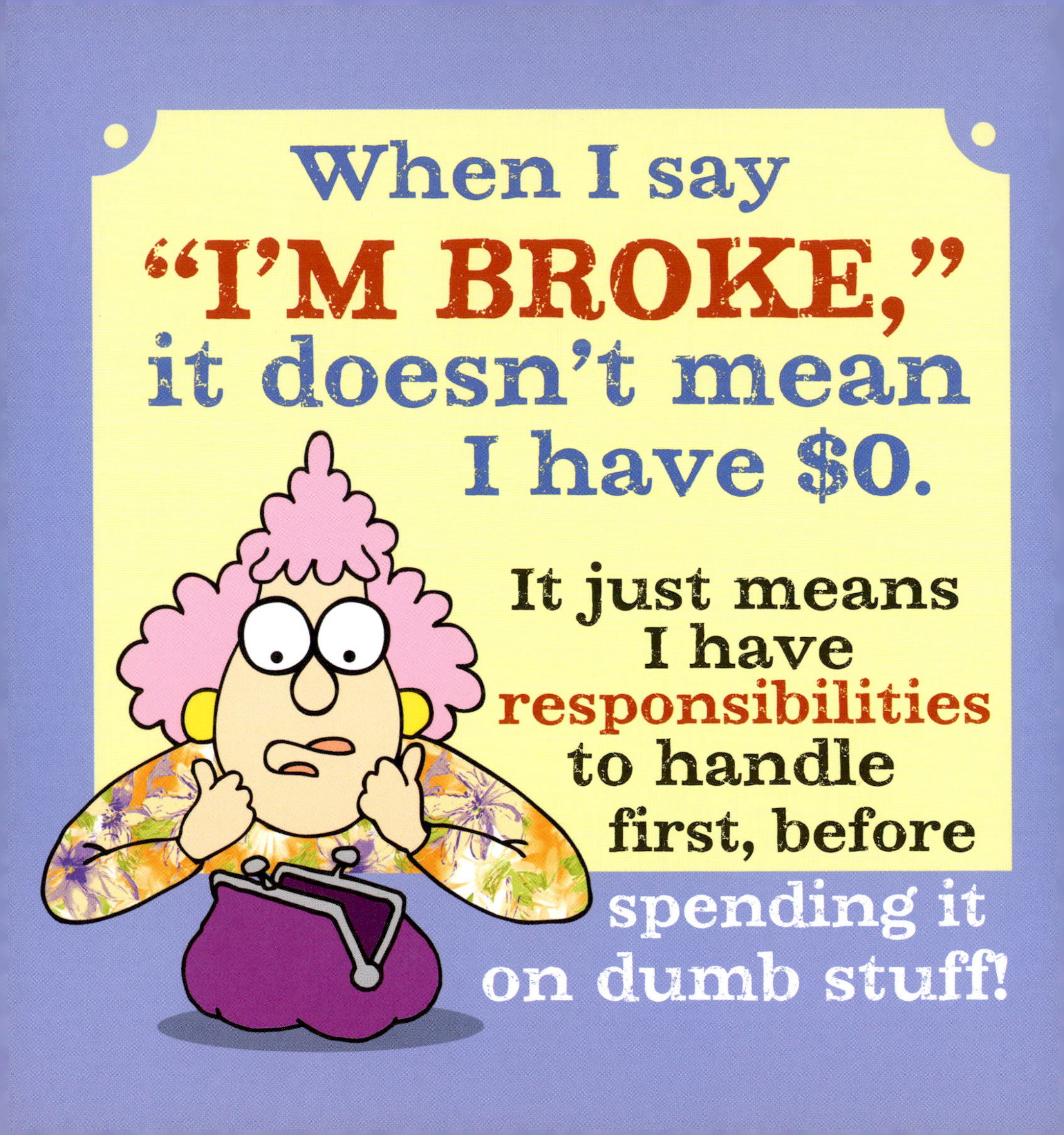

It just means
I have
responsibilities
to handle
first, before
spending it
on dumb stuff!

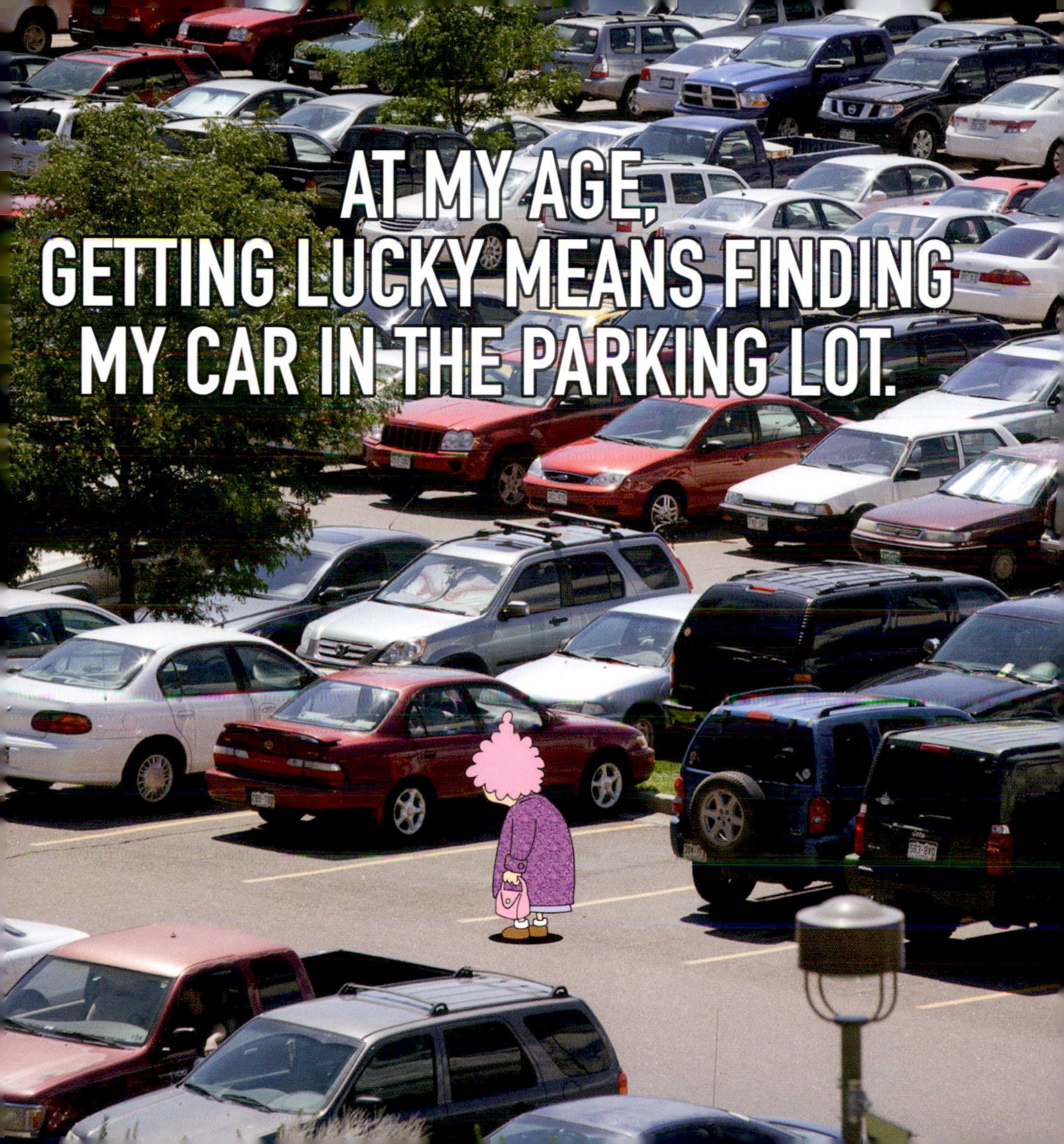
AT MY AGE,
GETTING LUCKY MEANS FINDING
MY CAR IN THE PARKING LOT.

IT'S ALL ABOUT ME! ME! ME!

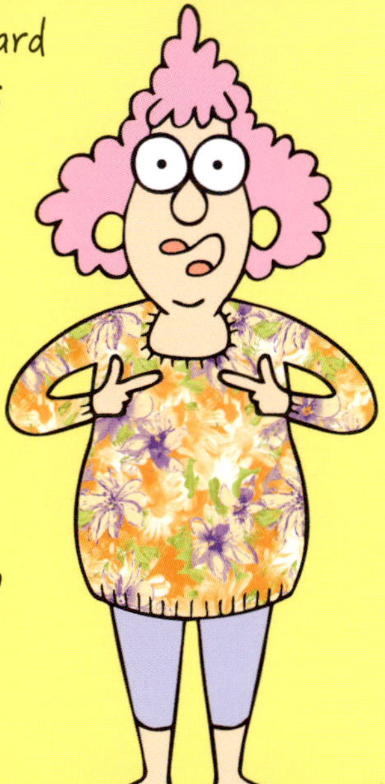

Forget all the rumors you might have heard about me; I'm an angel. Really, the horns are just there to make sure my halo sits straight. Of course, sometimes I have the occasional daydream of whipping it off and throwing it at someone's head, but would I actually ever hurt someone? Only if they were stupid enough to interrupt before my first sip of coffee of the freakin' day!

So, if you've ever wanted to get to know me a little better, my current CRAZY LEVELS, what makes me laugh and all about my fabulous QUEENDOM—flick the page—I'll be waiting for you!

ATTENTION:

I AM NOT BOSSY.

I am the QUEEN of this castle.

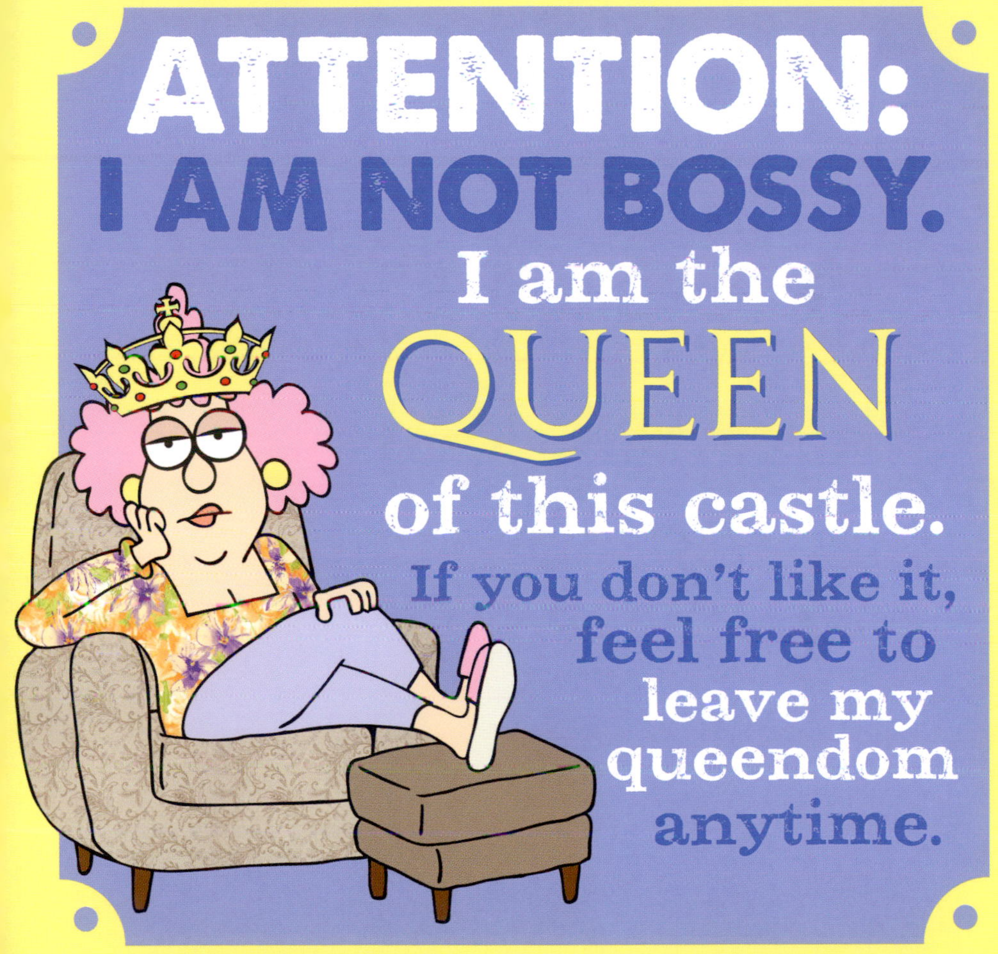

If you don't like it, feel free to leave my queendom anytime.

Just cleaned my **whole house** from top to bottom…

so now I'm gonna need everybody to stop living here.

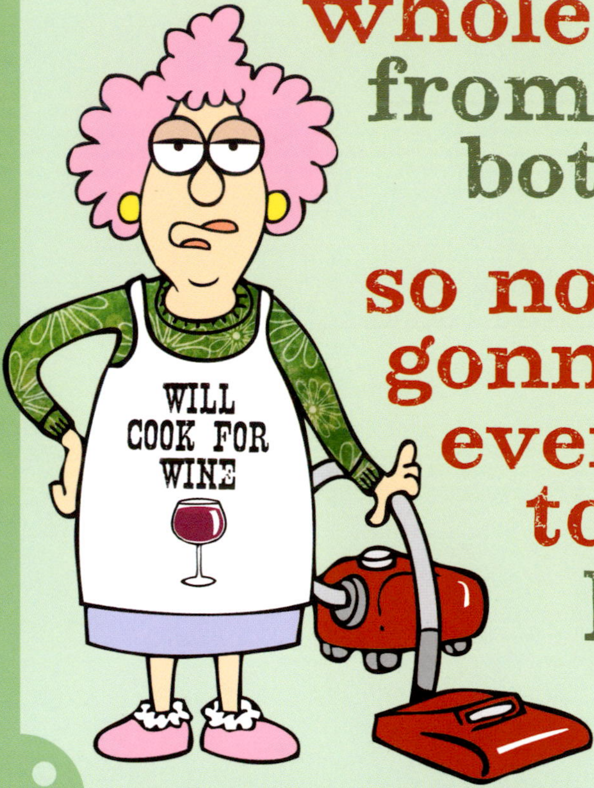
WILL
COOK FOR
WINE

My hobbies include: putting on my pajamas as soon as I get home.

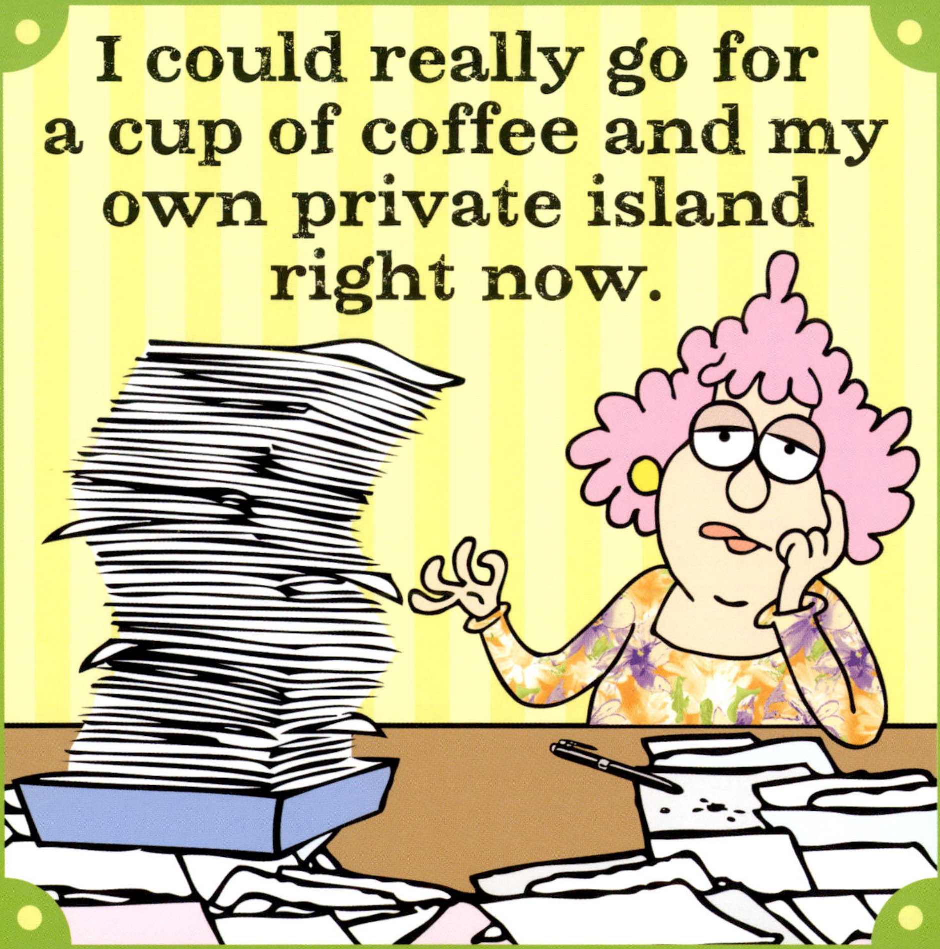
I could really go for a cup of coffee and my own private island right now.

I'll never be a good example... so I may as well be a fabulous warning!

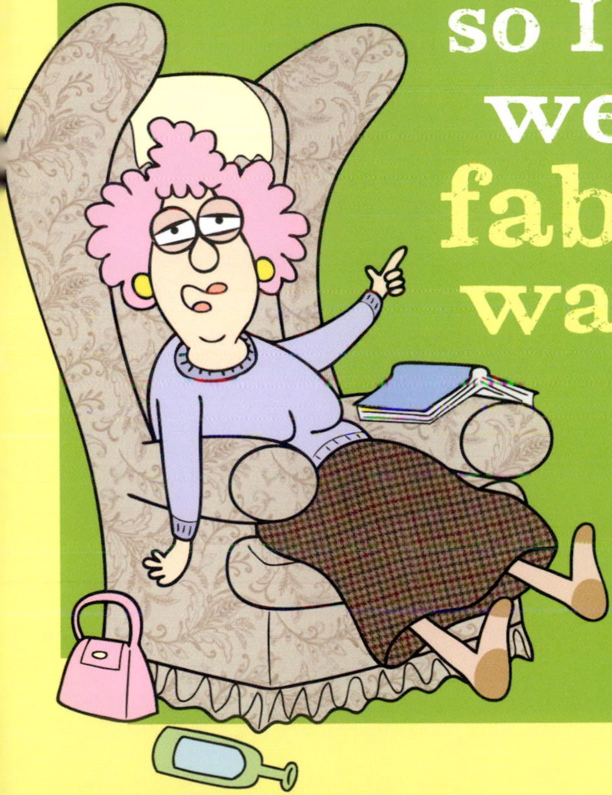

If you think I'm **Crazy** now... you should see me with my **best friend!**

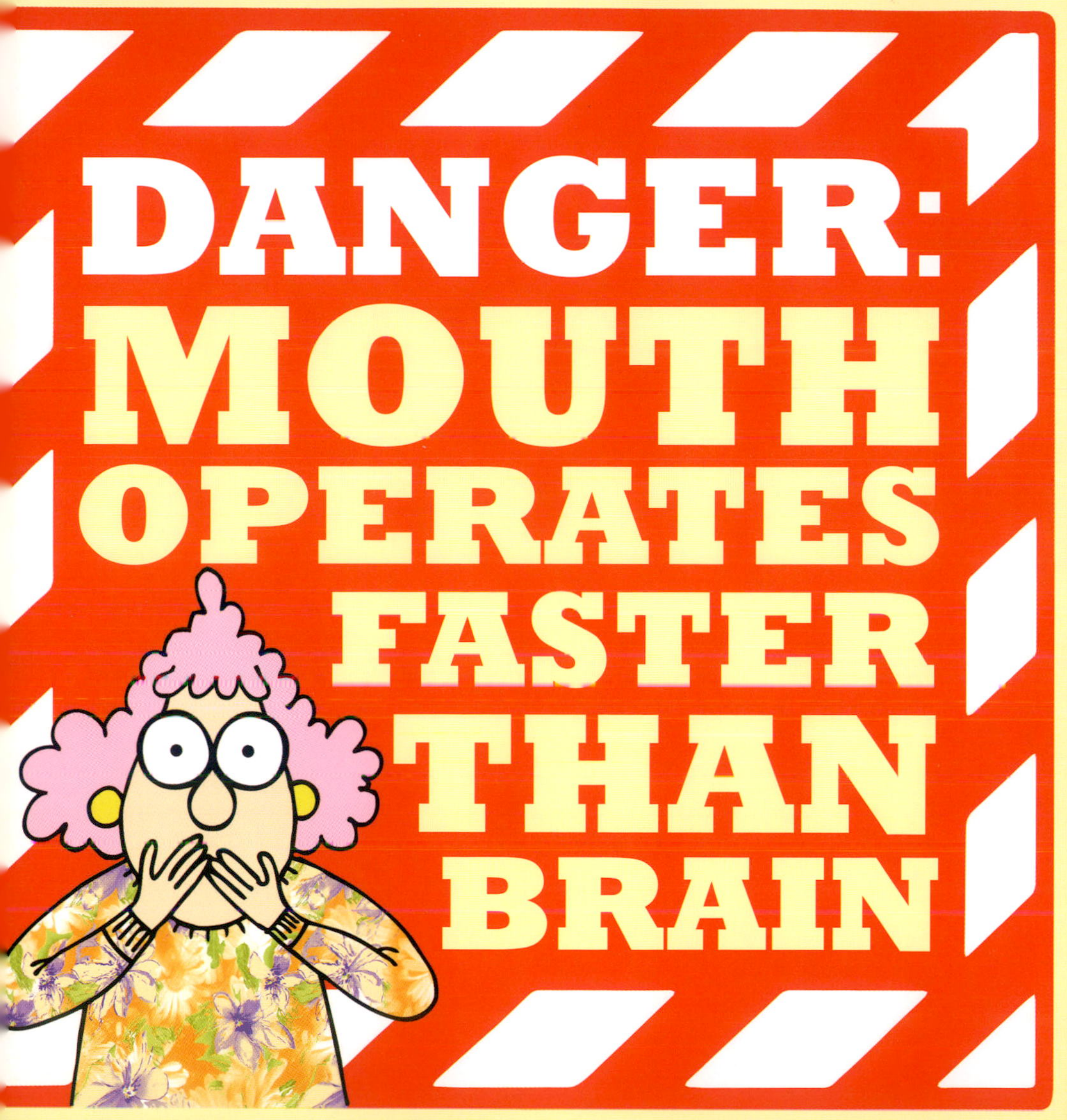
DANGER:
MOUTH
OPERATES
FASTER
THAN
BRAIN

I would like to say

thank you

to all the people
who came into
my life and made it
outstanding.

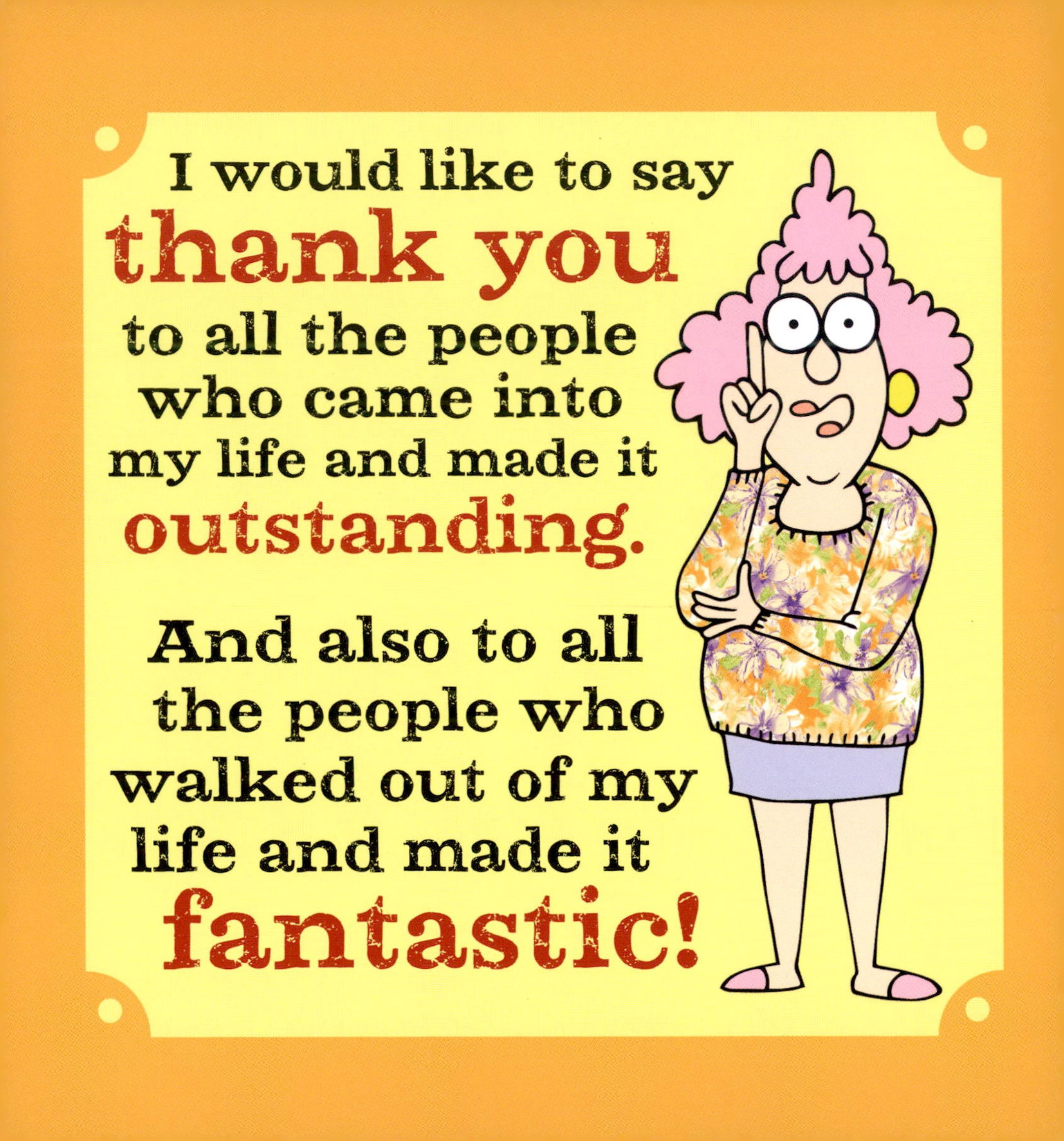

And also to all
the people who
walked out of my
life and made it
fantastic!

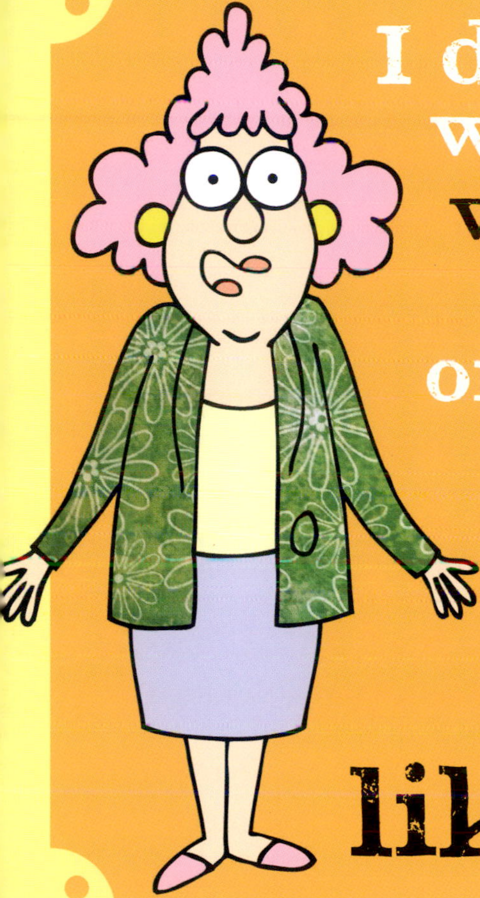

I don't care who you are, where you are from or what you look like. If you make me laugh, then I like you.

aunty acid's

THOUGHTS FROM THE TUB

Every time you've beaten a computer at chess, it's because it let you win.

Sawdust is just man glitter.

Thousands of years ago, books overtook tablets as the primary way to read. Now tablets are overtaking books.

If vampires can't see their reflections, why is their hair always so neat?

Our hair turning gray is like our bodies running out of ink.

Hand-cuffing a deaf person infringes upon their First Amendment rights.

Sheet music is like a sound recipe.

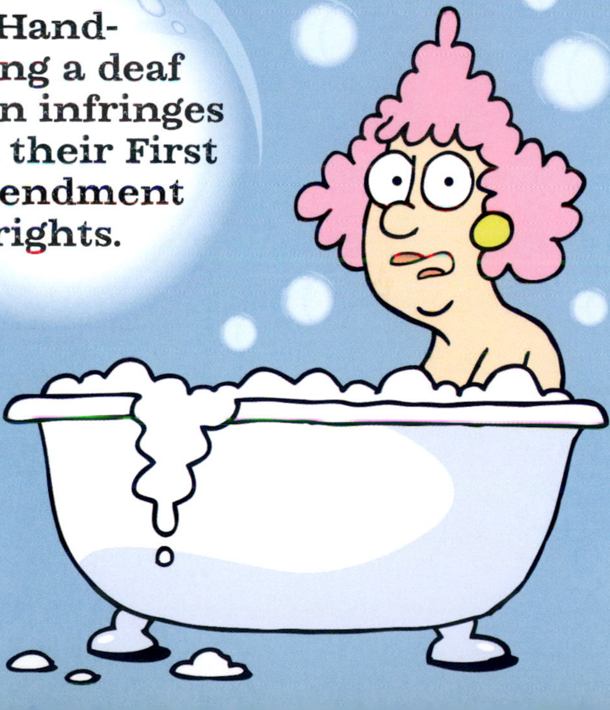

WORDS of WISDOM

I'm always getting caught talking to myself... sometimes I need expert advice! It can be hard to find at times; my brain is like my spare room—full to the ceiling with all sorts of crap! But between the stacks of old magazines and boxes of clothes that I've promised I'll freakin' fit into again, there are some gems of wisdom to be found. Well, I've mined my mind and dug out some nuggets of pure gold to give you some food for thought (not donuts unfortunately), and here they are—my famous Words of Wisdom!

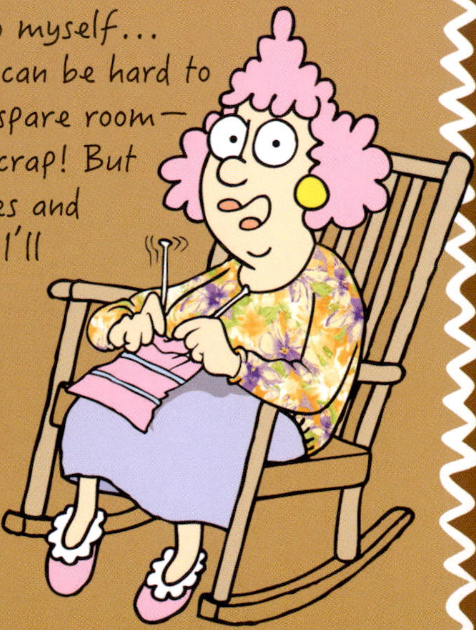

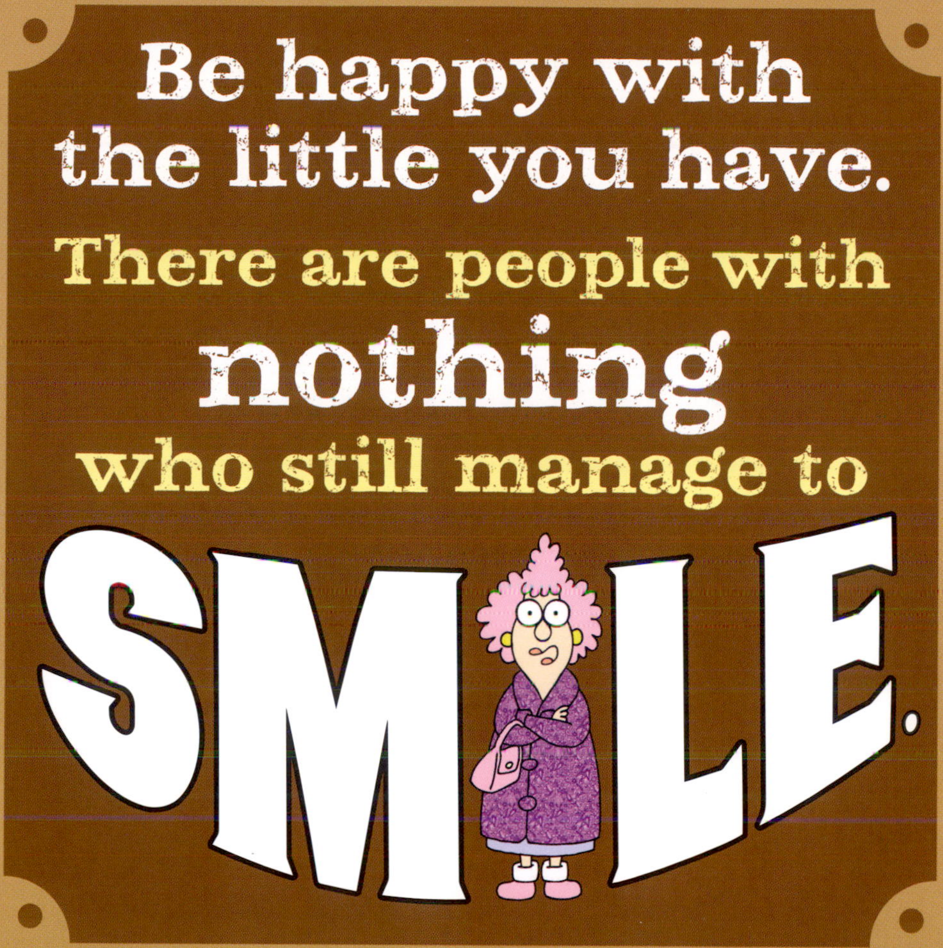
Be happy with
the little you have.
There are people with
nothing
who still manage to
SMILE.

Saying sorry never fixed anything. **You could try just** not being a jerk **instead.**

When one door closes...

sometimes you should get a **hammer and nails** to make sure the darn thing **stays shut!**

Don't wait until you're **rich** to be **happy.**

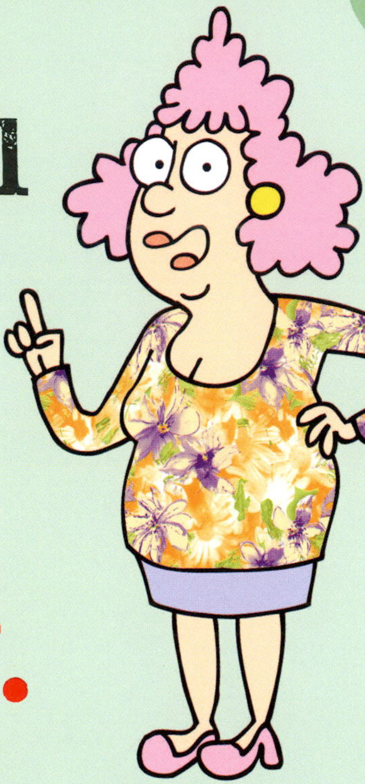

Happy is free.

Some people only

hate you
because
of the way
other
people
love you.

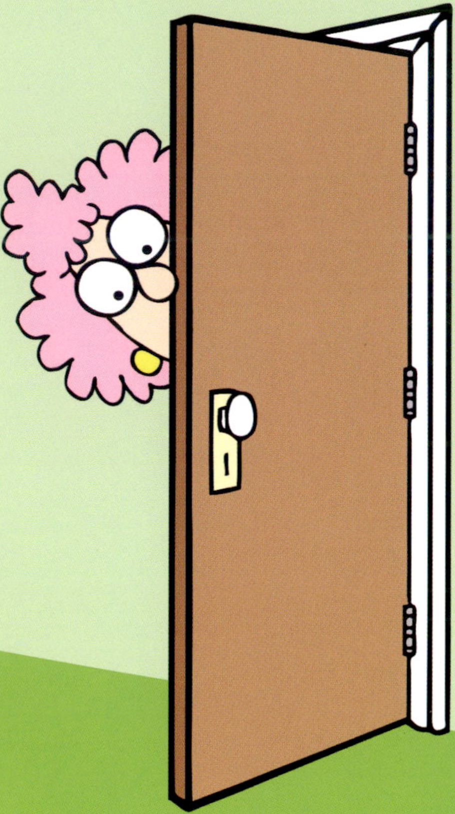

There is
nothing
to fear
but fear
itself

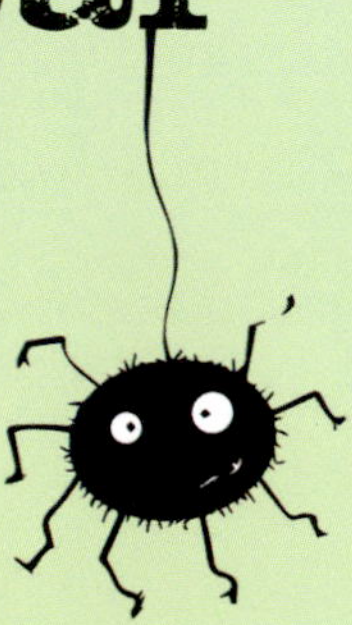

...and spiders!

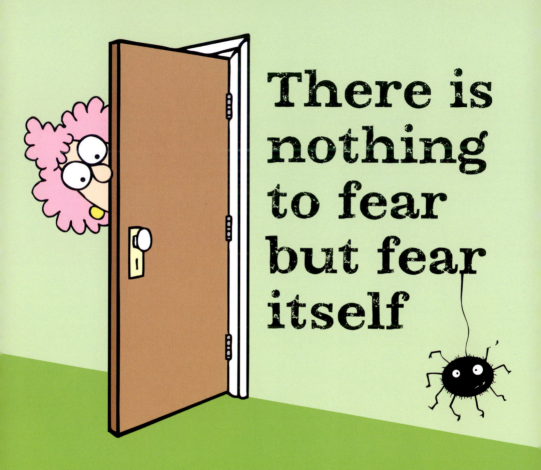

Whoever
is trying to
bring
you
down
is already
below
you.

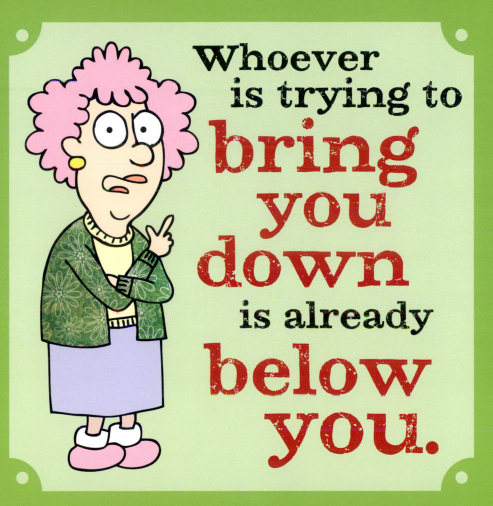

Common sense is not a gift; it's a punishment.

Because you have to deal with everyone who hasn't got it!

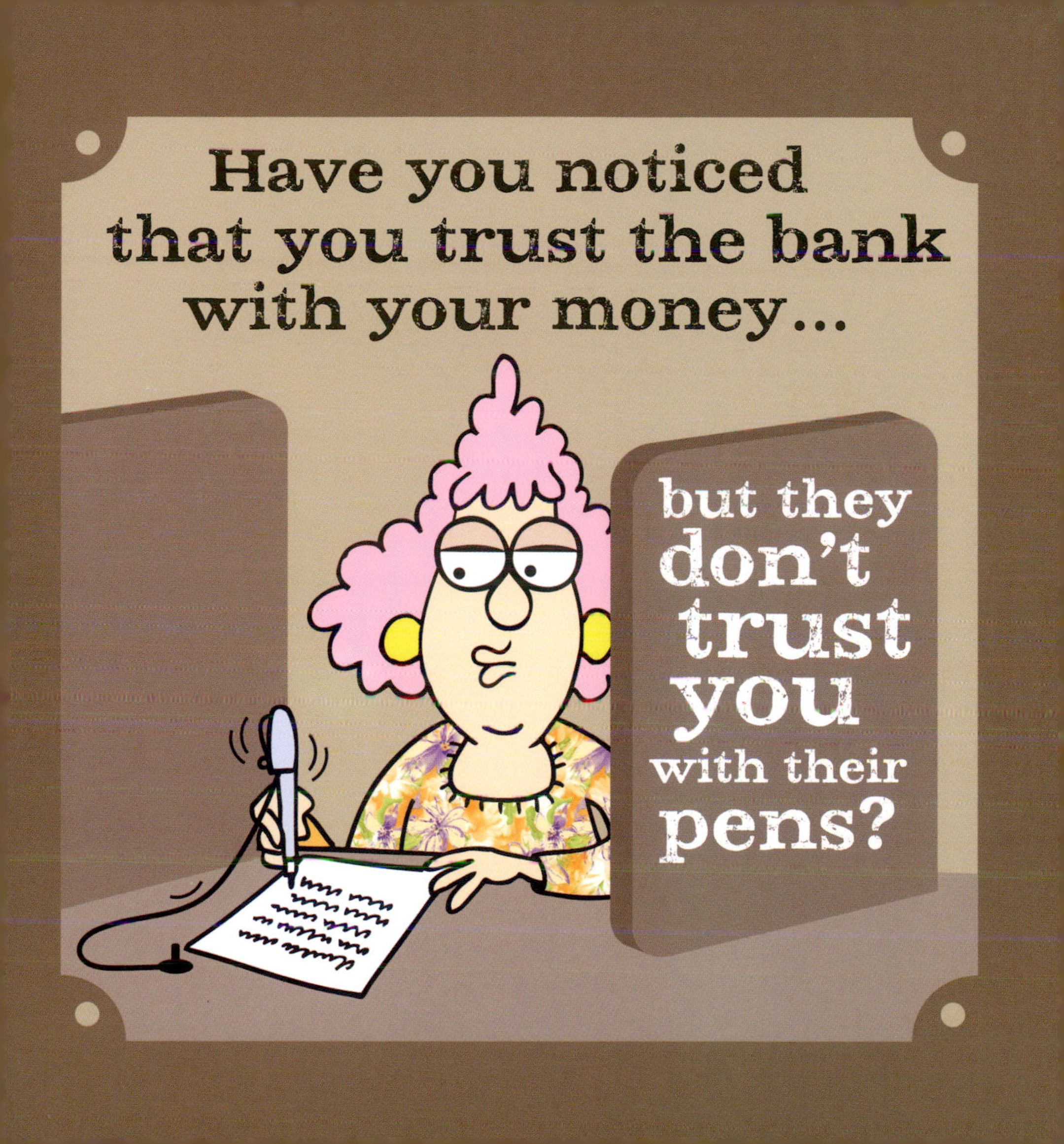
Have you noticed that you trust the bank with your money...
but they don't trust you with their pens?

If you don't like where you are...

MOVE.

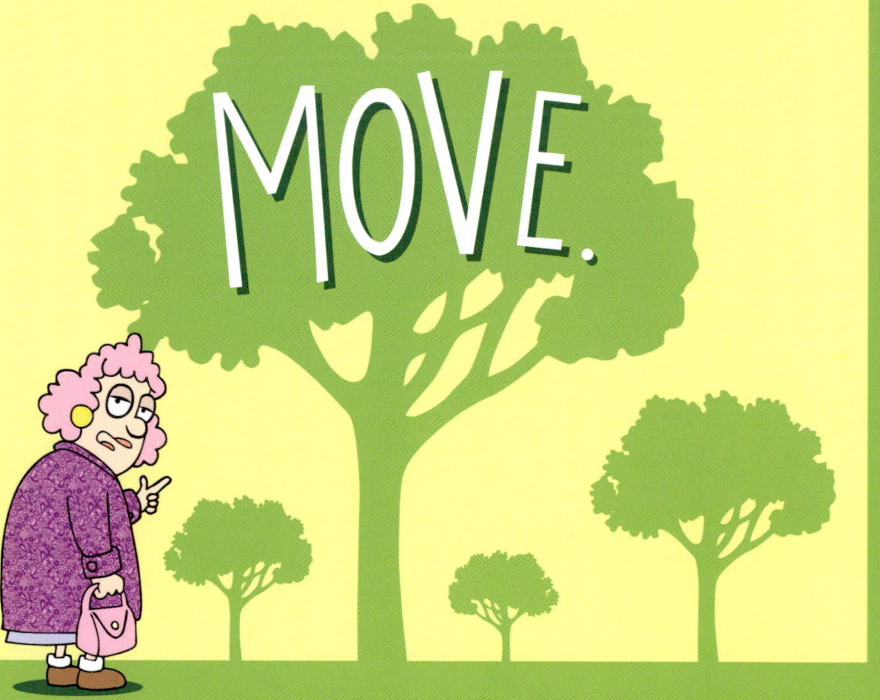

You're not a tree!

One day you'll just be a memory to some people.

Do your best to be a good one.

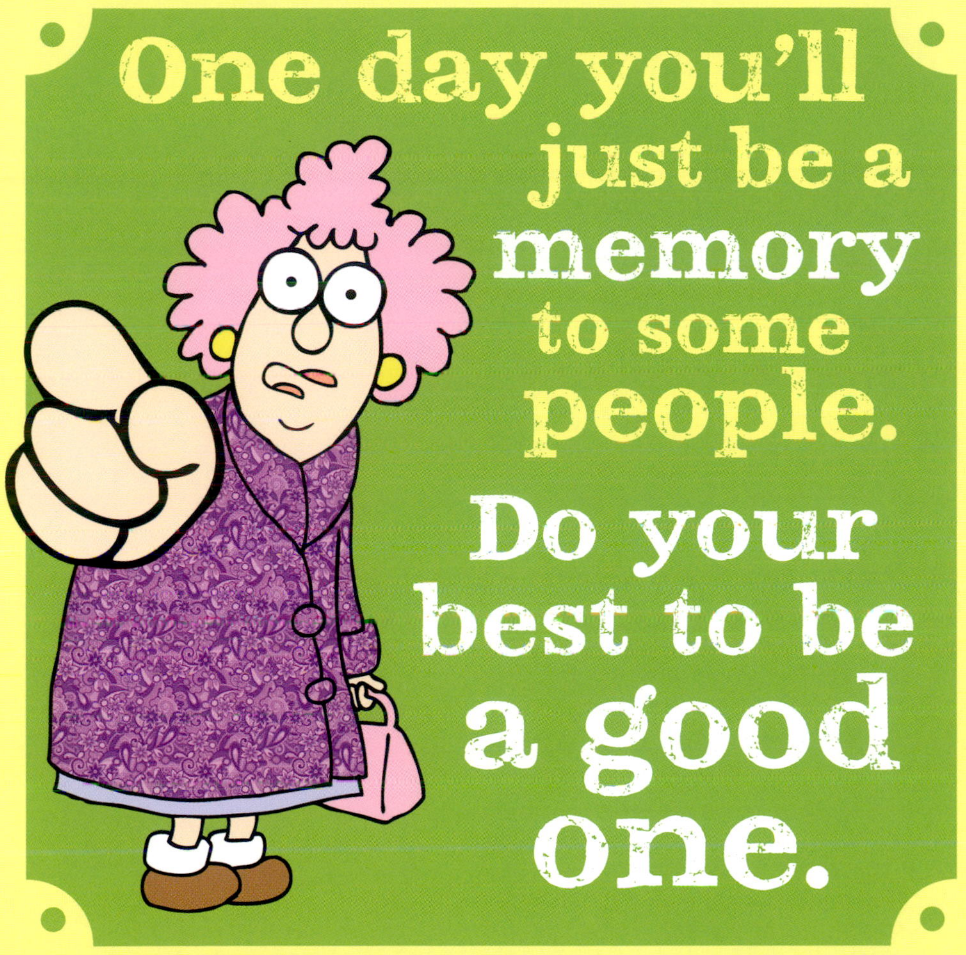

I stopped explaining myself when I realized people can only understand from their own level of stupidity.

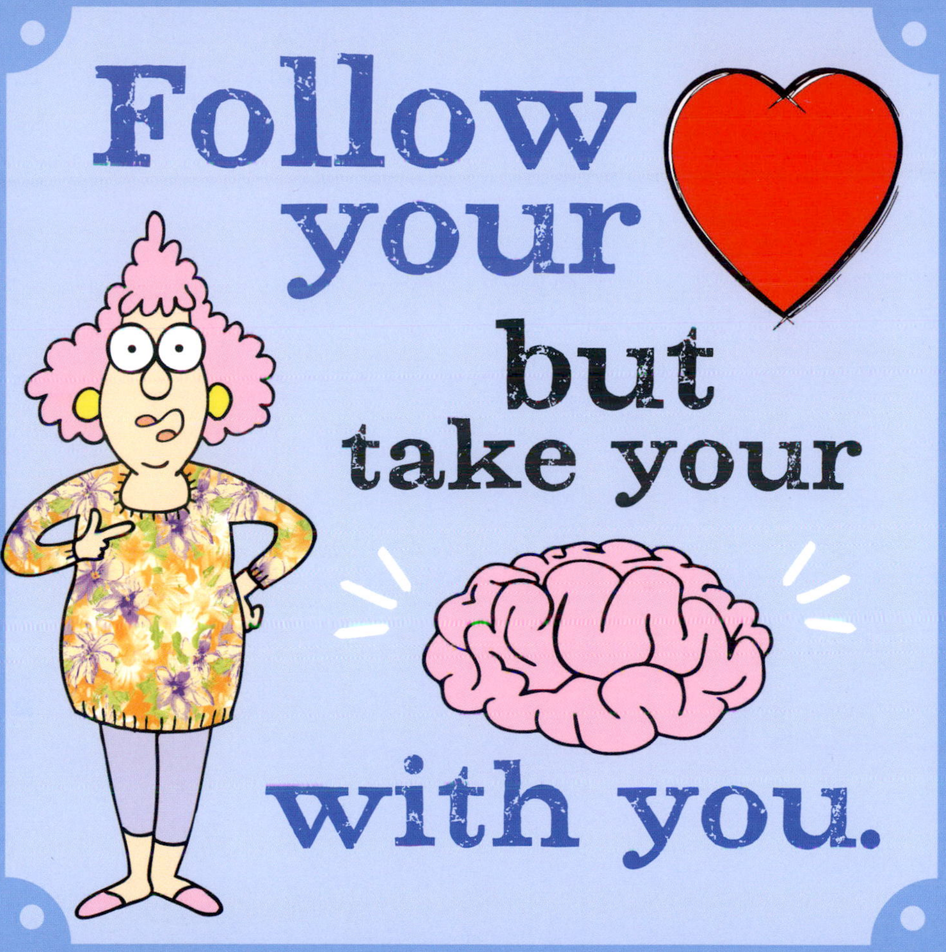
Follow your
but take your
with you.

First Edition
20 19 18 17   5 4 3

Cartoons © 2016 Ged Backland
Aunty Acid Characters created
by Ged Backland and Dave Iddon

All rights reserved. No part of this book may be
reproduced by any means whatsoever without written
permission from the publisher, except brief portions
quoted for purpose of review.

Published by
Gibbs Smith
P.O. Box 667
Layton, Utah 84041

1.800.835.4993 orders
www.gibbs-smith.com

Illustrations by
Dave Iddon @ Backland Media
Designed by Dave Iddon
Contributed material by
Raychel Backland & Stacey Thomas

Printed and bound in China
Gibbs Smith books are printed on
either recycled, 100% post-consumer
waste, FSC-certified papers or on
paper produced from sustainable
PEFC-certified forest/controlled wood
source. Learn more at www.pefc.org.

ISBN 13: 978-1-4236-4248-0